Death 24x a Second

Death 24x a Second

Stillness and the Moving Image

Laura Mulvey

REAKTION BOOKS

*Between past and future. For Zoe Wollen, born 2003, and in memory of her
great-grandmother Sylvia Mulvey, 1908–2000.*

Published by Reaktion Books Ltd
33 Great Sutton Street
London EC1V 0DX

www.reaktionbooks.co.uk

First published 2006

Printed and bound in Great Britain by Biddles Ltd, Kings Lynn

British Library Cataloguing in Publication Data
Mulvey, Laura
    Death 24 x a second: stillness and the moving image
    1. Motion pictures – Philosophy 2. Stills (Motion pictures)
    I. Title
    791.4'3'01

    ISBN–10: 1 86189 263 2

Contents

Preface

When I first started writing about cinema, in the early 1970s, films had always been seen in darkened rooms, projected at 24 (or thereabouts) frames a second. Only professionals, directors and editors had easy access to the flatbed editing tables that broke down the speed needed to create the illusion of 'natural' movement. By the end of the twentieth century ways of consuming cinema had multiplied and the regulation of its speed had been widely extended. Then, in the 1970s, I was preoccupied by Hollywood's ability to construct the female star as ultimate spectacle, the emblem and guarantee of its fascination and power. Now, I am more interested in the way that those moments of spectacle were also moments of narrative halt, hinting at the stillness of the single celluloid frame. Then, I was concerned with the way Hollywood eroticized the pleasure of looking, inscribing a sanitized voyeurism into its style and narrative conventions. Now, I am more interested in the representations of time that can be discovered in the relation between movement and stillness in cinema. Then, I was absorbed in Hollywood cinema, turning to the avant-garde as its binary opposite. Now, I think that the aesthetics of cinema have a greater coherence across its historic body in the face of new media technologies and the new ways of watching films that they have generated.

These contrasts between 'then' and 'now' are not intended to indicate a detachment from the past but rather to emphasize that my engagement with the cinema of the past has been changed by passing time. In the first chapter of this book, I discuss ways of looking back to the past but through an altered perspective, informed by the problems and possibilities of the present. My point of departure is an obvious, everyday reality: that video and digital media have opened up new ways of seeing old movies. The unexpected encounters that emerge out of this meeting of technologies are familiar to anyone who has experimented with them, from film scholar to film fan. But behind this initial engagement between present and past lies a more rhetorical one. A return to the cinema's past constitutes a gesture towards a truncated history, to those aspects of modernist thought, politics and aesthetics that seemed to end prematurely before their use or relevance could be internalized or exhausted. These histories have been deeply interwoven with the history of cinema. Such a return to the past through cinema is paradoxically facilitated by the kind of spectatorship that has developed with the use of new technologies, with the possibility of returning to and repeating a specific film fragment. Return and repetition necessarily involve interrupting the flow of film, delaying its progress, and, in the process, discovering the cinema's complex relation to time. Needless to say, there is nothing fundamentally new here. To see cinema through delay is to discover a cinema that has always been there, either overtly in the experiments of the avant-garde or more covertly in the great range of fiction film.

In this sense, this book is about a changed perspective, the way that my perception of cinema has changed between 'then' and 'now' and the way that, within the context of the present, the representation of time has taken on new significance. My examples and discussion of, for instance, stillness are drawn as much from the cinema of the past as they are drawn from new mechanisms of delay. Delayed cinema works on two levels: first of all it refers to the actual act of slowing down the flow of film. Secondly it refers to the delay in time during which some detail has lain dormant, as it were, waiting to be noticed. There is a loose parallel here with Freud's concept of deferred action (*nachtraglichkeit*), the way the unconscious preserves a specific experience, while its traumatic effect might only be realized by another, later but associated, event.

Freud developed his thoughts on deferred action out of his analyses of the problem of sexuality in human development. A small child might well not understand the significance of a sexual encounter or witnessed event. Later, however, after the onset of sexual maturity, a similar experience may reactivate the significance of this memory, forgotten and stored in the unconscious. The cinema (like photography) has a privileged relation to time, preserving the moment at which the image is registered, inscribing an unprecedented reality into its representation of the past. This, as it were, storage function may be compared to the memory left in the unconscious by an incident lost to consciousness. Both have the attributes of the indexical sign, the mark of trauma or the mark of light, and both need to be deciphered retrospectively across delayed time.

In common with other film theory today, this book is heavily marked by the image of, and the questions raised by, the photographic index. While technology never simply determines, it cannot but affect the context in which ideas are formed. Inevitably, the arrival of digital technology has given a new significance to the representation of reality and precipitated a return to the semiotic theory of the index. In the semiotic system elaborated by C. S. Peirce, an icon is a recognizable sign. It refers to the 'thing' it represents through similarity. A symbol is a decipherable sign; it refers to the 'thing' it represents by means of conventions or codes. An index, however, is a sign produced by the 'thing' it represents. An indexical sign might be recognizable through similarity, as, for instance, in a footprint, and thus have shared qualities with the icon. Or it might be decipherable through a code, as, for instance, in the shadow cast by a sundial, and thus have shared qualities with the symbol. But something must leave, or have left, a mark or trace of its physical presence. Whether it persists, as in the then-ness of a preserved fingerprint, or not, as in the now-ness of a sundial's shadow, the 'thing' inscribes its sign at a specific moment of time. Thus, the index has a privileged relation to time, to the moment and duration of its inscription; it also has a physical relation to the original of which it is the sign. While the photographic image, in semiotic terms, usually includes the iconic and often includes symbolic aspects of the sign, its aesthetic specificity is grounded on the index. The photograph cannot generalize. While written (symbolic) or graphic (iconic) representations can evoke a class of things, a photographic image is always of one specific and unique, although, of course, endlessly reproducible, thing. A return to the index and to the real of the photographic medium is not a return to realism's aspiration to certainty. Rather, the trace of the past in the present is a document, or a fact, that is preserved in but also bears witness to the elusive nature of reality and its representations. It is here that the reality of the photograph as index becomes entwined with the problem of time.

These semiotic terms recur across this book as I try to reformulate my thoughts on spectatorship through the perspective of time and the varying temporalities inherent in film itself. At certain points in my argument these questions lead to those associated with modes of address that locate verbal exchange in time and place. These words (called 'shifters' by Roman Jakobson) indicate a speaker's own specific point of utterance in space and time, so, for instance, 'now' can refer only to the moment at which it is spoken. Due to this exact reference to an exact position, these words function as 'indicators' and share the indexical sign's embedding in time and place. But as part of a symbolic system, language, they are infinitely flexible and transferable, so that one person's 'here' becomes another person's 'there'. These ideas are central to the chapter 'The Index and the Uncanny' but are further elaborated in the last three chapters of the book in the context of 'The Possessive Spectator' and 'The Pensive Spectator'. But more generally, the context for the thoughts reflected in this book is located across the space between the shifter words 'then' and 'now', with which I began this Preface.

As an index, cinema necessarily fixes a real image of reality across time. As I hope to establish in the first three chapters of this book, however, the very reality of the index creates uncertainty. First of all, any factual raw material arouses, or should arouse, a practical sense of uncertainty in terms of its interpretability. The index is a material trace of something and as it depends for meaning, by and large, on secondary iconic and symbolic signs, it is easily overwhelmed or betrayed. But an amorphous, more intangible, difficulty arises out of the presence of preserved time. The cinema combines, perhaps more perfectly than any other medium, two human fascinations: one with the boundary between life and death and the other with the mechanical animation of the inanimate, particularly the human, figure. These porous boundaries introduce the concept of the uncanny and Freud's debate with Jentsch about the power of the old over the new and the hold that irrational belief has over the human mind. The first part of the book discusses these kinds of ways in which reality cannot escape the human unconscious. Necessarily embedded in passing time, these images come to be more redolent of death than of life. These themes recur throughout the book's central section and are discussed in the context of the three central case histories.

In the final section of the book I discuss the pensive and possessive spectators that emerge from a delayed cinema. The pensive spectator is more engaged with reflection on the visibility of time in the cinema; the possessive spectator is more fetishistically absorbed by the image of the human body. But this differentiation is deceptive and recalls Christian Metz's observation that the intellectual spectator cannot be detached from fetishism. In his analysis of the cinema fetishist ('the person enchanted by what the cinema is capable of', its technological equipment), Metz points out:

> Indeed, the equipment is not just physical (= the fetish proper); it also has its discursive imprints, its extensions into the very text of the film. Here is revealed the specific movement of theory: when it shifts from a fascination with technique to the critical study of the different codes that this equipment authorises. Concern for the signifier in the cinema derives from a fetishism that has taken up its position as far as possible along its cognitive flank. To adapt the formula by which Octave Mannoni defines disavowal (= 'I know very well but all the same'), the study of the signifier is a libidinal position

which consists in weakening the 'but all the same' and profiting from this saving of energy to dig deeper into the 'I know very well' which then becomes 'I know nothing at all, but I desire to know'.[1]

The fetishistic spectator and the libidinal student of the signifier may well be one, but, at a certain point, a desire to know comes to the fore, if only to fold back into its previous position. The deferred look may be unexpectedly overwhelmed by images of time that stop individual desires in their tracks as they stumble across the 'I know nothing at all, but I desire to know'.

Cinema, as it ages, has become more and more the object of 'I desire to know', most obviously in the expansion of film and related studies over the last 25 years, but also through the new availability of old cinema through new technology. At the same time, cinema's aesthetic polarities, debated throughout its critical history, seem to become less important in their differences and more important in their dialectical relations with each other. Rather than diverging into an either/or, for instance, specificity of the filmstrip versus illusion of movement, fiction versus document, grounding in reality versus potential for fantasy, these aspects of the celluloid-based medium move closer together. Passing time, in and of itself, shifts perception of relations and aesthetic patterns and these shifts are, in turn, accentuated by the new horizons formed by new technologies. As a result, a new kind of ontology may emerge, in which ambivalence, impurity and uncertainty displace the traditional oppositions. Above all, it is essential to emphasize that these shifts in theory and criticism are the result of a displaced perspective and deferred action. The cinema has always found ways to reflect on its central paradox: the co-presence of movement and stillness, continuity and discontinuity.[2] To look back into the cinema's history, out of passing time and refracted through new technology, is to discover a medium in which these kinds of uncertainties have constantly recurred. In the aesthetic of delay, the cinema's protean nature finds visibility, its capacity to create uncertainty that is, at the same time, certainty because its magic works without recourse to deception or dissimulation. The cinema renders, in Dziga Vertov's words, 'uncertainty more certain'.

I would like to conclude this Preface with a reflection on a well-known section of Vertov's *Man with a Movie Camera*, which has been, throughout the writing of this book, a constant companion and source of visual pleasure for me. The sequence begins as the cameraman films a carriage drawn by a white horse as it canters down a Moscow street, ferrying passengers from the railway station to their home. At a moment when the horse fills the frame, the film freezes into a still 'photograph'. The build-up to this moment, the spectator realizes retrospectively, had been geared around movement. The sequence had been prefigured by a shot of a train taken from track level that concentrated the energy of the machine leading into the rapid movement of the carriage, and the horse in particular. This accumulation of movement had carried forward the movement of the film and of time itself, so when the image froze another temporal dimension suddenly emerged. While movement tends to assert the presence of a continuous 'now', stillness brings a resonance of 'then' to the surface. Here, Vertov manages to switch these registers with a single image. The sequence also leads on to a consideration of the relation and difference between the stilled image and the filmstrip.

Despite the fact that *Man with a Movie Camera* is a documentary, recording the streets of Moscow in 1929, and despite the fact that any filmed image has the same indexical status as the image stilled, the sense of temporality attached to film and to photography differ. This is not simply a matter of movement and stillness, but of the single image as opposed to the filmstrip, the instant rather than the continuum. The reality recorded by the photograph relates exclusively to its moment of registration; that is, it represents a moment extracted from the continuity of historical time. However historical the moving image might be, it is bound into an order of continuity and pattern, literally unfolding into an aesthetic structure that (almost always) has a temporal dynamic imposed on it ultimately by editing. The still photograph represents an unattached instant, unequivocally grounded in its indexical relation to the moment of registration. The moving image, on the contrary, cannot escape from duration, or from beginnings and ends, or from the

The film freezes into a still 'photograph', from *Man with a Movie Camera* (Dziga Vertov, 1929).

The film frame: singularity and sequence.

Two kinds of time blend together.

patterns that lie between them. The still image of the horse suggests a photograph. It asserts the moment at which that one frame was recorded, even as it is duplicated to create a freeze effect. But the sequence continues and explores the single frame's place in the sequence rather than in isolation.

Vertov takes this exposition further. The sequence moves to other freeze frames (the surrounding streets, faces of women and children from this and other sequences) and then introduces the celluloid strip itself. When the image of a child is shown repeated in the individual frames of a fragment of film the sequence seems to touch the point between the aesthetic of photography and the cinema. In their stillness, the repeated images belong to the photograph, to the moment of registration, but in their sequence they signify poignantly the indivisibility of these individual moments from a larger whole, an integral part of the shift into movement. They represent the individual moments of registration, the underpinning of film's indexicality. In Jean-Luc Godard's film of 1960, *Le Petit Soldat*, the answer to the question 'what is cinema?' is 'truth 24 times a second'. But these frames as individual photographs are also a testament to cinema's uncanny. So the answer to the question 'what is cinema?' should also be 'death 24 times a second'. The photograph's freezing of reality, truth in Godard's definition, marks a transition from the animate to the inanimate, from life to death. The cinema reverses the process, by means of an illusion that animates the inanimate frames of its origin. The shots of filmstrips lead into the editing room where Elizaveta Svilova is working on *Man with a Movie Camera*. She holds the inert filmstrip in her hands; she winds it on the editing table; she cuts out certain frames. The inanimate frames come back to life; people from very different sections of the movie look, react, tellingly including the faces of children who will be found much later watching a magic show. Finally the continuum of the film is reestablished with its own temporal logic, in which the question of time constantly occurs, but within its own unfolding structure. In this sequence, the editor's work personifies the reordering and transforming of raw material. As she sets the filmstrip back into motion on the editing table the moving image gradually reintegrates the sequence back into the course of the film. But the spectator is brought back with a heightened consciousness of the blending of two kinds of time.

Vertov concentrates concisely and elegantly into a few minutes many of the ideas that I have tried to articulate in this book. This reflection on two kinds of time explores the relations between movement and stillness in the cinema long before new technology made them easily accessible. But Vertov's delayed cinema is a reminder across time, across the decades of the twentieth century, of the aesthetic and political relation between film and modernity. With a repetition of deferred action, the return to the cinema of the 1920s that was so influential in the 'then' of the 1960s and '70s has, perhaps, even more relevance in the present climate of political and aesthetic dilemma.

Chapter One
Passing Time

In 1995 the cinema celebrated its 100th birthday. Critics, theorists, historians and even the public at large suddenly focused their attention on the current 'state of the cinema'. Centenaries bestow a symbolic significance on the centenarian: transitions, upheavals, mutations become visible and debatable. Suddenly, the cinema seemed to age. Furthermore, in the opinion of professional archivists and conservationists, celluloid had proved to be an essentially short-lived material, with chemical decay an inherent part of its physical make-up. According to Paolo Cherchi Usai: 'Moving image preservation will be redefined as the science of gradual loss and the art of coping with the consequences, very much like a physician who has accepted the inevitability of death even while he fights for the patient's life.'[1] Aged 100, the cinema had also been inevitably affected by the natural mortality of the human figures whose existences it unnaturally preserved. More and more has cinema come to be a memorial to those who personified its modernity, its glamour, its triumph as both a popular form and an art form. The institutions of its maturity had, some time before the centenary, grown old as its stars, directors and production systems retired, died and declined. Chris Petit comments in his video *Negative Space* (1999): 'The cinema is becoming increasingly about what is past. It becomes a mausoleum as much as a palace of dreams.' As time passes, these ghosts crowd around the cinema as it its own life lies in question and the years around the centenary saw the death of the last great Hollywood stars. In 2004 Marlon Brando followed in the wake of Katherine Hepburn, who followed in the wake of Gregory Peck. To see the star on the screen in the retrospectives that follow his or her death is also to see the cinema's uncertain relation to life and death. Just as the cinema animates its still frames, so it brings back to life, in perfect fossil form, anyone it has ever recorded, from great star to fleeting extra.

Elegiac reflections on the cinema's ageing found substance in a more immediate, material and objective change as mechanical and chemical technology gave way, gradually, to the electronic and, more dramatically, to the digital. The year 1997 saw the first marketing of film on digital format.[2] The resonance of ageing, and of death, associated with the cinema's centenary coincided with the arrival of a technology that created a divide between the 'old' and the 'new' media. However significant the development of video had been for film, the fact that all forms of information and communication can now be translated into binary coding with a single system signals more precisely the end of an era. The specificity of cinema, the relation between its material base and its poetics, dissolves while other relations, intertextual and cross-media, begin to emerge. Furthermore, the digital, as an abstract information system, made a break with analogue imagery, finally sweeping away the relation with reality, which had, by and large, dominated the photographic tradition. The sense of the end of cinema was thus complicated aesthetically by a crisis of the photographic sign as index. Although a photograph may have other properties, the physical link between an object caught by a lens and the image left by rays of light on film is the material basis for its privileged relation to reality.

The technological drive towards photography and film had always been animated by the aspiration to preserve the fleeting instability of reality and the passing of time in a fixed image. The problem would always be how to hold on to images made by the concentration of light, how to inscribe their reality indexically and mechanically. Human imagination has always been enthralled by the magical aspect of this kind of mechanical reproduction. Cinema and photography belong to the long tradition of 'natural magic', as the Jesuit Athanasius Kircher called his experiments with the camera obscura in the mid-seventeenth century. Kircher had mastered the optics necessary to concentrate rays of light, to project images from the world outside onto a screen inside a darkened room and reverse the inverted image with mirrors. He could show moving images of whatever happened outside, the landscape, sometimes casual passers-by, sometimes staged, complex set pieces. Needless to say, the images could not be fixed or preserved and the camera obscura's cumbersome technology could not be realized as a medium with actual market potential. In quite another tradition, the magic lantern, with its man-made illusions, captured the early entertainment market and was the main site for the research and development from which the cinema finally emerged. It was the chemical fixing of the optically focused image that enabled the invention of the photograph and 'natural magic' swept back into visual culture. Ultimately the legacy of the camera obscura was realized in the cinema, but its images, like photography, unlike the camera obscura, could appear only as the result of a delay, a detour into the chemical process of development and printing. Furthermore, unlike the camera obscura's actual presentation of reality, of real movement and of the passing of real time, the cinema created an illusion of movement, as a series of stills appear animated at the correct number of frames per second.

Whatever their limitations, photographic machines register the image inscribed by light on photosensitive paper, leaving the trace of whatever comes in front of the lens, whether the most lavishly constructed of sets or the most natural of landscapes. While the photographic machine may reflect and inflect the image as human imagination constructs or desires, it still remains indifferent, a recording mechanism detached from the human eye. In the 1990s digital technology brought back the human element and man-made illusions. The story of mechanical, photographic, reproduction of reality came to an end. The conversion of recorded information into a numerical system broke the material connection between object and image that had defined the earlier history. No longer derived from the chemical reaction between light and photosensitive material, these images lost their 'natural magic' and the painterly character of the illusions of the magic lantern, the tradition of human ingenuity, returned to visual culture. Lev Manovich describes this return:

> The manual construction of images in digital cinema represents a return to nineteenth century pre-cinematic practices, when images were hand-painted and hand-animated. At the turn of the twentieth century, the cinema was to delegate these techniques to animation and define itself as a recording medium. As cinema enters the digital age, these techniques are again becoming commonplace in the film making process. Consequently, cinema can no longer be distinguished from animation. It is no longer an indexical media technology but, rather, a sub-genre of painting.[3]

This revolution in image culture and technology might well seem to put the seal of closure on the more amorphous sense of an end signalled by the cinema's centenary. As Lev Manovich puts it, 'Cinema is the art of the index; it is an attempt to make art out of a footprint.'[4] However lacking in artistic aspiration the footprint may be, as an indexical sign it marks an actual moment in time as well as the shadowy presence of an event as potentially significant, for instance, as Friday's arrival on Crusoe's island.

The artist Jeff Wall has brought the 'manual' back into his photographic work, while, in a number of his pictures, also incorporating the aesthetic and emotional resonance of the index. In *A Sudden Gust of Wind (After Hokusai)* (1993), his re-creation of a Hokusai print, he combines a tribute to artists' longstanding pre-photographic aspiration to capture a precise moment in time with a technique drawn from the more 'painterly' potential of the digital. In both pictures, the wind has suddenly caught four passers-by on a little bridge. One turns to watch his hat blow sky high alongside an 'arabesque' of floating papers torn from the hands of another. In terms of photographic history, the scene depicts the kind of decisive moment at which a photographer's eye and a fleeting second of movement are brought together as, for instance, in Cartier-Bresson's famous photograph of a man caught by the camera as he is reflected in mid-jump over a puddle. At first glance *A Sudden Gust of Wind* possesses this quality that the Hokusai original aspired to. But on further consideration the photograph seems to go, in a strange way, beyond the instant it represents. It seems to be too visually complex, and too theatrical in its gestures.

Rather than catching a decisive moment, *A Sudden Gust of Wind* pays tribute to the aesthetic concept of the indexically caught instant through a detour into non-indexical technology. The scene is staged, as though in a tableau, and its details further perfected through digital enhancement. Although this combination of camera and computer is common enough both in contemporary media in general and in Wall's work in particular, the picture dramatizes the dialogue between the two. Through the very introduction of staging and manipulation, a celebration of photography's unique inscription of time is turned into a reflection on photographic time, especially its apotheosis as frozen movement. As Wall brings simulation to the aesthetic of reality, he gives the picture a theoretical dimension reflecting a transitional moment in which both technologies coexist, in which the aesthetic of the digital still thinks with the idea of the index. At the same time, with this citation of Hokusai, Wall reaches back to a 'painterly', nineteenth-century, depiction of the 'decisive moment'.

The threat of extinction, of course, draws new attention to the index and its present pathos retrospectively affects the vast body of film and photographic material that has accumulated over the last century and a half. Now, as old films that were conceived and shot on celluloid are re-released in constantly increasing numbers on DVD, the two media, the old and the new, converge. The new technology offers an opportunity to look back to the 'before', to the 'then' of the indexical image, in the changing light of the 'after', the 'now'. The aesthetics of the past meet the aesthetics of the present, bringing, almost incidentally, new life to the cinema and its history. But this new life (movies reissued and restored, new modes of consumption) also transforms the ways in which old films are consumed. Once upon a time, most people could only watch a movie in the cinema where it was projected at the correct pace for the illusion of movement and according to a given narrative sequence. Now, cinema's stillness, a projected film's best-kept secret, can be easily revealed at the simple touch of a button, carrying with it not only the suggestion of the still frame, but also of the stillness of photography. On one side, that of pre-cinema, stands the photograph. The image is still, but, like film, it is indexical. On the other side, that of post-cinema, stands the digital, unlike the cinema in its material composition but able to carry the mechanical, celluloid-based moving image into a multi-media future. But the post-cinematic medium has conjured up the pre-cinematic. Like the central panel of a triptych that has blurred at the edges, the cinema reaches both forwards and backwards. But at point of convergence between the old and the new, the easily accessible freeze frame brings the presence of death back to the ageing cinema. The still, inanimate, image is drained of movement, the commonly accepted sign of life.

Throughout the history of cinema, the stilled image has been contained within the creative preserve of the film-maker, always accessible on the editing table and always transferable into a freeze frame on the screen. It was video, arriving in the late 1970s and gaining ground during the 1980s, that first extended the power to manipulate the existing speed of cinema. Although the instability of the electronic image undercut the exhilaration that these experiments brought with them, the accumulated experience of the last video-dominated decades can be carried into the digital age. But the present context has further heightened the significance of this new interactive spectatorship. A dialectical relationship between the old and new media can be summoned into existence, creating an aesthetic of delay. In the first instance, the image itself is frozen or subjected to repetition or return. But as the new stillness is enhanced by the weight that the cinema's past has acquired with passing time, its significance goes beyond the image itself towards the problem of time, its passing, and how it is represented or preserved. At a time when new technologies seem to hurry ideas and their representations at full tilt towards the future, to stop and to reflect on the cinema and its history also offers the opportunity to think about how time might be understood within wider, contested, patterns of history and mythology. Out of this pause, a delayed cinema gains a political dimension, potentially able to challenge patterns of time that are neatly ordered around the end of an era, its 'before' and its 'after'. The delayed cinema gains further significance as outside events hasten the disappearance of the past and strengthen the political appropriation of time.

Five years after the cinema's centenary, another date intervened. The millennium generated a flurry of speculation about temporal markers of a more historical and general kind. Other divisions between past and future, the nature of an era and its end eclipsed the story of the cinema's demise. Because of the arbitrary, purely mythological significance of the date, the year 2000 always seemed inadequate to sustain the hype that surrounded it. But in other ways the millennium concentrated into itself a widely perceived sense of change that had built up over the previous two decades, for instance the impact of the end of communism, the advance of globalization, the shift in communication technologies, the decline of industry in the developed world. From this perspective, a resonance of change, of breaks with the past, could be associated with the year 2000. The mythology, that is, happened to coincide with a period of accelerated political and economic upheaval and crisis. As Angela Carter had observed with characteristic wit some twenty years earlier, 'The *fin* is coming a little early this *siècle*.' It only took a subsequent gestation period of a year and nine months for apocalypse to catch up with the millennium. With the events of September 2001 in New York and Washington, DC, the indistinct sense of foreboding that belonged to the year 2000 found an emblematic embodiment. Politicians, journalists and cultural commentators of all kinds argued that the world had been irrevocably changed. The threads of continuity woven through twentieth-century history and modernity that had been loosened over its last decades by theories of postmodernism and 'the end of history' seemed definitively cut. The twentieth century receded even more rapidly into the past, out of synchrony with the newly configured present. This linear concept of time attempts to divest itself of past residues, overtly wiping clean the slate of history even as earlier eras struggle to survive.

The question of how history acquires pattern and shape has political significance and the rush of new technology towards the future, its indifference to the past, may fall into step with the new conservatism. In this context, the cinema, rather than simply reaching the end of its era, can come to embody a new compulsion to look backwards, to pause and make a gesture to delay the combined forces of politics, economics and technology. The cinema's recent slide backward into history can, indeed, enable this backward look at the twentieth century. In opposition to a simple determinism inherent in the image of a void between the 'before' and the 'after' of an era that had suddenly ended, the cinema provides material for holding onto and reflecting on the last century's achievements as well as learning from its catastrophes. To turn to the past through the detour of cinema has a political purpose. Jean-Luc Godard's *Histoire(s) du Cinéma* (1998), his extraordinary reflection on the cinema's own history, entwined with its recording of the history of the twentieth century, is emblematic of such a move. He produced *Histoire(s)* during the transitional period of the 1980s and '90s, working with different technologies and aesthetics, reflecting on cinema as an art and as popular culture, as politics and as industry. But, most particularly, Godard draws attention to the stretch of celluloid imagery across the twentieth century, its presence as an inscription of history, even through its silences, distortions, repressions. The history of the *Histoire(s)* does not produce cinema as history pure and simple, but as raw material that can be the site of reflection and contestation.

Antoine de Becque sees Godard's work as a fitting end to a twentieth century that, he argues, began with *The Train Entering the Station* (Lumière Brothers 1895). 'If you haven't seen *Histoire(s)*, you've missed the century's exit', and he continues:

> this is the ultimate lesson to be learnt from *Histoire(s)*: the imaginary museum is also an embodied museum, i.e., the cinema has made

flesh the history of the century. It could also take ideas, references, works, concepts so as to enable the century to think. It is an embodied body and a corpus: for the century, cinema has been and is still a tangible surface revealing history and the knowledge of where to seek its great representations.[5]

But de Becque's pattern of the century could be reformulated, placing *Histoire(s)* rather as a new beginning, prefiguring ways in which cinema will increasingly become a source of collective memory of the twentieth century for those who missed living through it.

Eric Hobsbawm describes the point at which personal memory disappears into history as the 'twilight zone'.[6] On celluloid, personal and collective memories are prolonged and preserved, extending and expanding the 'twilight zone', merging individual memory with recorded history. The passing of time affects the cinema, and the presence of the past, even in a fiction film, may suddenly distract the spectator from its story line. Siegfried Kracauer, writing in the 1950s, reflects on the way that cinema materializes memory unexpectedly onto the screen:

> As he laughs at [old films], however, he is bound to realise, shudderingly, that he has been spirited away into the lumber-room of his private self . . . In a flash the camera exposes the paraphernalia of our former existence, stripping them of the significance that originally transfigured them so they are changed from things in their own right into invisible conduits.[7]

He describes this sense of being revisited by the past as it is channelled through film into the present, precipitating the kind of involuntary memory that itself confuses time:

> The thrill of these old films is that they bring us face to face with the inchoate, cocoon-like world from which we come – all the objects, or rather the sediments of objects, that were our companions in a pupa state . . . Numerous films . . . draw on the incomparable spell of those

near and far away days which mark the border region between the present and the past. Beyond it the realm of history begins.[8]

While the coincidence between the cinema's centenary and the arrival of digital technology created an opposition between the old and the new, the convergence of the two media translated their literal chronological relation into a more complex dialectic. Everyone knows that celluloid consists of a series of still frames that have been, by and large, inaccessible to the film spectator throughout its history. Digital technology enables a spectator to still a film in a way that evokes the ghostly presence of the individual celluloid frame. Technically this is an anachronism. It is only due to an imaginative association with film's archaic structure that the materiality of celluloid comes to mind. But the imaginative association can lead to intellectual and aesthetic reverie as the delay in the film's flow acts as a 'conduit', in Kracauer's phrase, that then flows into multiple possible channels from personal memory to textual analysis to historical research, opening up the past for a specifically cinematic excavation. But the delay, the association with the frame, may also act as a 'conduit' to the film's uncertain, unstable, materiality torn between the stillness of the celluloid strip and the illusion of its movement, leading to further reflection on the representation of time, particularly in relation to the index. Here again, the technology has rendered the presence of the index anachronistic, but its already ghostly presence can enhance reflection on the actual filmic image under consideration, its presence as an inscription of a moment of time. The dialectic between old and new produces innovative ways of thinking about the complex temporality of cinema and its significance for the present moment in history. As the flow of cinema is displaced by the process of delay, spectatorship is affected, reconfigured and transformed so that old films can be seen with new eyes and digital technology, rather than killing the cinema, brings it new life and new dimensions. The process of delay not only brings stillness into visibility but also alters the traditionally linear structure of narrative, fragmenting its continuities.

Changes in the technologies of seeing affect human perception. As so many theorists and film-makers argued in the 1920s,
the cinema, with its mechanical eye, embodied ways in which
modernity had transformed perception. Now, as the digital affects
contemporary perception of the world, so it also affects popular
experience of film and the mode of perception traditionally associated with it. In the first instance, computer-generated images create
a 'technological uncanny', the sense of uncertainty and disorientation which has always accompanied a new technology that is not
yet fully understood. As digital production has merged the human
and other bodies seamlessly into special effects the 'technological
uncanny' has given way to 'technological curiosity' and DVDs
include 'add-ons' with background information, interviews and
commentaries. These extra-diegetic elements have broken through
the barrier that has traditionally protected the diegetic world of
narrative film and its linear structure. Furthermore, as a DVD indexes
a film into chapters, the heterogeneity of add-ons is taken a step
further by non-linear access to its story. Of course, these new
features also enhance understanding of the movies of the past,
shifting them from pure entertainment into a quasi-museum-like
status. While more and more people, beyond the specialized film
buffs, fans and cinephiles of the past, are plunged into film history,
the experience is far removed from that of the traditional cinema
audience bound to watch a film in its given order at 24 frames a
second. In this dialogue between old and new, past and present,
the opposition between film and new technologies begins to break
down and the new modes of spectatorship illuminate aspects of
cinema that, like the still frame, have been hidden from view.

Once the consumption of movies is detached from the
absolute isolation of absorbed viewing (in the dark, at 24 frames a
second, in narrative order and without exterior intrusions), the
cohesion of narrative comes under pressure from external discourses, that is, production context, anecdote, history. But digital
spectatorship also affects the internal pattern of narrative:
sequences can be easily skipped or repeated, overturning hierar-
chies of privilege, and setting up unexpected links that displace the

chain of meaning invested in cause and effect. This kind of interactive spectatorship brings with it pleasures reminiscent of the processes of textual analysis that open up understanding and unexpected emotion while also attacking the text's original cohesion. When broken down in this way, a movie's apparently horizontal structure mutates, so that symmetry or pattern can be detached from the narrative whole or a privileged moment can suddenly take on the heightened quality of a tableau. And then, some detail or previously unnoticed moment can become at least as significant as the chain of meaning invested in cause and effect. In the stilled image, moments of beauty or meaning can be found and then, as the image is reactivated, continue to affect the image once returned to movement.

In his introduction to *The Remembered Film*, Victor Burgin draws attention to the way that viewing processes once embraced by the avant-garde have shifted so that the Surrealists' habit of moving from cinema to cinema to create arbitrary sequences and juxtapositions is now transformed into the commonplace:

> During the more recent history of cinema, less self-consciously resistant practices have emerged in the new demotic space that has opened up between the motion picture palace and consumer video technologies . . . Moreover, even the most routine and non-resistant practice of 'zapping' through films shown on television now offers the sedentary equivalent of Breton's and Vaché's ambulatory *dérive*. Their once avant-garde invention has, in Victor Shklovsky's expression, 'completed its journey from poetry to prose. The decomposition of narrative films, once subversive, is now normal.'9

He points out that this disruption of the linear recalls other kinds of mental processes. As well as the unconscious associative links in a dream's latent material, in daydreams and reveries, the mind travels across unexpected, apparently arbitrary chains of association that may or may not be ultimately comprehensible when recalled to the conscious mind. As he discusses the way in which memory can detach a film sequence from its larger narrative and give it a stronger connection with a sequence from another film, he says:

> The narratives have dropped away like those rockets that disintegrate in the atmosphere once they have placed their small payloads in orbit. Detached from their original settings, each scene is now the satellite of the other. Each echoes the other, increasingly merges with the other, and I experience a kind of fascinated incomprehension before the hybrid object they have become.[10]

Not only does Burgin give an illuminating insight into the way film moments can work in the psyche, he also draws attention to the way that film material can be literally detached from its original site to become part of the creative material of contemporary artists. References to film have been significant in his previous work, but his latest, *Listen to Britain*, evolves out of and around a sequence from Powell and Pressburger's *A Canterbury Tale*. If watching films digitally has contributed to a sense of narrative disintegration, digital editing systems have enabled film to be quoted and referred to with unprecedented ease. Once again, like the Surrealists' *dérive*, such references are not necessarily new but have found heightened visibility in the digital era. Furthermore, as the cinema ages it acquires greater cultural legitimacy and the divide between art and popular film has narrowed almost to invisibility.

In Burgin's account of the way that a film image or sequence can become part of a network of other images or ideas in a 'non-linear concatenation', the Freudian model of unconscious association is never far way. Anna Everett draws on Julia Kristeva's theory of intertextuality to discuss similar properties of digital culture, devising the term 'digitextuality':

> Where digitextuality departs from Kristeva's notion of intertextuality is that the former moves us beyond 'a new signifying system' of quotations and transpositions to a meta-signifying system of discursive absorption whereby different signifying systems are translated and

often transformed into zeros and ones for infinite recombinant signifiers. In other words, new digital media technologies make meaning not only by building a new text through translation and absorption of other texts, but also by embedding the entirety of other texts (digital and analogue) seamlessly within the new. What this means is that earlier practices of collage, bricolage and other modernist and postmodernist hybrid representational strategies and literary gestures of intertextual referentiality have been expanded for the new demands and technological wizardry of the digital age.[11]

Both Burgin and Everett locate the non-narrative strategies that have developed out of the digital within the traditions of the avant-garde, within an aesthetic of the synchronic or even the achronic. Similarly, the digital 'freeze frame' recalls the importance that reference to the single frame of film has had in the avant-garde tradition. But the implications are double-edged. While stillness indeed challenges film's appropriation by illusion, the digital freeze frame can only refer to the film's material, the frame, by associations that lie outside the specifics of the medium so central to modernist aesthetics.

Thinking about film within the framework of the digital is like watching a kaleidoscope pattern reconfigure very slowly. The same aesthetic attributes are there but the relations between them have shifted. For instance, the oppositions between narrative and avant-garde film, between materialism and illusion, have become less distinct and the uncertain relation between movement and stillness, and between halted time and time in duration, is now more generally apparent. Rather than stripping away a mask of illusion to reveal film's material, the relation between film's attributes can be reformulated more dialectically. This affects the opposition between 'film time', the inscription of an image onto the still frames of celluloid, and 'cinema time', the structure of significance and flow that constitutes the temporal aesthetic of any movie, fiction or documentary. Usually, the second conceals the first, but when the forward movement is halted the balance changes. The time of the film's original moment of registration can suddenly burst through its narrative time. Even in a Hollywood movie, beyond the story is the reality of the image: the set, the stars, the extras take on the immediacy and presence of a document and the fascination of time fossilized overwhelms the fascination of narrative progression. The now-ness of story time gives way to the then-ness of the time when the movie was made and its images take on social, cultural or historical significance, reaching out into its surrounding world. At moments like these, images from film culture (documentary, fiction, avant-garde) mix on equal terms with those from films of record (public, such as newsreels, or private, such as home movies). As Everett points out, bits of 'film time' can be extended and remixed out of their original cinematic context. Again, this development is only a further advance in the long tradition of the compilation film.

Looking back, the life-span of film and photography as the predominant media of their era has been comparatively short, bounded by a defined beginning, the fixing of the indexical image, and end, the perfect imitation of the indexical image by digital technology. The mechanical, even banal, presence of the photographic image as index takes on a new kind of resonance, touched perhaps by nostalgia, but no longer tied to old debates about the truth of photographic evidence. The index can now be valued in its relation to time and as a record of a fragment of inscribed reality that may be meaningless or indecipherable. As a trace of the past that persists into present, and one in which, in the case of the cinema, appears to animate the inanimate human body, the photographic index reaches out towards the uncanny as an effect of confusion between living and dead. Human consciousness creates ordered time to organize the rhythms of everyday life according to the demands of society and economy, but also in recognition of the intractable nature of time itself. For human and all organic life, time marks the movement along a path to death, that is, to the stillness that represents the transformation of the animate into the inanimate. In cinema, the blending of movement and stillness touches on this point of uncertainty so that, buried in the cinema's materiality, lies a reminder of the difficulty of understanding passing time and, ultimately, of understanding death. As Raymond Bellour puts it:

> If the stop on the image, or of the image, what one might also call the photographic 'take' on film, the pose or pause of the image asserts the power of stillness to enthral, if this impression is so strong, it must be because it touches the stop of death . . . [12]

He goes on to argue that the stop of death is also the moment of its suspension, the point at which the certainty of death is over-whelmed by enigma and uncertainty.

These attributes of cinema, although noted since its birth, were intensified by the transitional period of 1995 that brought with it the metaphor of the cinema's own death, further exaggerated by the new ease with which the cinema can be delayed. As stillness intrudes into movement, the image freezes into the 'stop of death', taking the aesthetics of cinema that leads back to pre-cinema, and to photographic and psychoanalytic theories. The blurred boundaries between the living and the not-living touch on unconscious anxieties that then circulate as fascination as well as fear in the cultures of the uncanny. This shudder, however consciously experienced, is a symptom of the unconscious difficulty that the human mind has in grasping death and its compensatory capacity to imagine an afterlife.

Chris Petit's tribute to the stars of *Journey to Italy* (1999).

George Sanders
1906–1972

Ingrid Bergman
1915–1982

Chapter Two

Uncertainty: Natural Magic and the Art of Deception

The cinema is descended from two, contradictory, ancestral lines that combined to make it the first ever medium to fulfill the longstanding aspiration to show moving images of the real world. Its relation to reality is, of course, shared with photography, and comes from the tradition of the camera obscura, while its movement belongs to the tradition of optical illusions that exploit a peculiar ability of the human eye to deceive the mind. Contained in this ancestry is a scientific drive to understand the eye, optics or light. But this scientific drive fed into new kinds of popular entertainment. As the economic and social conditions for a popular culture emerged during the nineteenth century, magicians and illusionists developed 'the arts of deception', appealing to human fascination with the unnatural, the impossible and, ultimately, the supernatural. The ideological mode of address adopted by these entrepreneurs would change over time. The dangerous, forbidden activities involved with summoning up the devil and his tricks gave way to other kinds of beliefs that, over and over again, tapped into the wide and changing variety of superstitions and beliefs associated with life after death. The cinema concentrated into itself a range of these pre-existing forms of illusion and entertainment.

Illusions of the supernatural typically bring into play peculiarities of both human vision and the human mind. A mind bewildered by optical and other kinds of illusions, doubting the reality of what it sees with its own eyes, is more prepared to be credulous when exposed to the emanations of the supernatural. An otherwise confident and competent relation to the world is suddenly faced by a sense of uncertainty. Whatever ideology or commercial enterprise might fuel these phenomena, they share an aesthetic of deception, an appeal to the human mind's pleasure in illusion and its constant readiness to be fooled. The machines of deception necessarily had a complex relation to the different ideologies within which they functioned, veering between complicity with irrational belief and its debunking. As they unveiled the workings of their illusions, the magicians 'demystified' the ways in which human credulity could always be exploited. In the aftermath of the Enlightenment, the world of the sacred was in retreat, so that pleasure in the irrational could emerge from religion into culture, as, for instance, in the early nineteenth-century cult of the Gothic. Even as the last shreds of superstition and religion seemed to retreat into the past, some irreducible core of human irrationality persisted. Freud's great contribution to modernity was to recognize that the irrational was intrinsic to human reason, 'housed' in the unconscious. While, in the first instance, the problem of sexuality structures the Freudian unconscious, it is also colonized by irrational fears, and that most rational of fears: the inevitability of death that lies 'beyond the pleasure principle'. Although there was no mutual interest, there is a coincidence of chronology in the 1890s between Freud's ambition to find ways of analysing the irrational and the arrival of the cinema. Cinema gathered together and streamlined its prehistory of illusion and deception by means of 'natural magic', giving modernity a perfect site on which to play out the continuing dramas of reality, the unconscious and the imagination.

The convergence between the arts of reality and the arts of deception that brought about the birth of the cinema in 1895 prefigures the convergence between the cinema machine and digital technology from 1997 that seemed to signal its death. Georges Méliès stands at the first, nineteenth-century, crossroads. A professional magician at the end of a long line of illusionists, Méliès brought cinema to magic, merging the two traditions and embodying the family relation between them. Méliès had two moments of epiphany in his life. The first took place at Maskeleyne's perma-

The Lumière Brothers: the magic of passing time. *A Boat Leaving the Harbour* (1895).

Georges Méliès: magic and the cinema. *A One Man Band* (1900).

nent magic theatre, the Egyptian Hall, in London in 1888, where he fell in love with magic, and, on his return to Paris, took over the theatre of the famous prestidigitator Jean-Eugène Robert-Houdin (after whom Houdini later named himself). The second was at the Lumière brothers' demonstration of the cinematograph in 1895 at the Grand Café in Paris, when he is said to have exclaimed: 'What a great trick! That's for me!' He then created a film studio that fused the new, cinematic potential for trickery with the traditions of the magic theatre.

In 1951 the Surrealists published a list dividing the history of the cinema into two opposed columns of names.[1] The Lumières headed one list, 'Don't See'; Méliès headed the other, 'See'. For the Surrealists, the Lumière brothers' cinema was tied to the banal realm of realism, while Méliès could conjure up a parallel universe of surreal magic and marvellous effects. Looking back, after more than a century since the advent of cinema, this opposition no longer seems so simple. Both cinemas now have associations with the marvellous. It is impossible to see the Lumière films as a simple demonstration of a new technology; every gesture, expression, movement of wind or water is touched with mystery. This is not the mystery of the magic trick but the more disturbing, uncanny sensation of seeing movement fossilized for the first time. This uncanny effect was also very vividly present for the cinema's first spectators; the images' silence and lack of colour added to their ghostly atmosphere. Maxim Gorky's well-known response to the Lumière films bears witness to this, as he wrote in 1896 for a Russian newspaper: 'It is terrifying to watch but it is the movement of shadows, mere shadows. Curses and ghosts, evil spirits that have cast whole cities into eternal sleep come to mind and you feel as though Merlin's vicious trick had been played out before you.'[2]

As cinema technology became integrated into everyday life and its workings were no longer mysterious, the Lumières' films were overtaken by the banality of their reality like any home movie or technological demonstration, to be dismissed by the Surrealists. But now, after more than a hundred years, the further passing of time has created a third phase and that very reality has become the source of uncanniness. The phantom-like quality observed by Gorky and his contemporaries returns in force. The inanimate images of the filmstrip not only come alive in projection, but are the ghostly images of the now-dead resurrected into the appearance of life. These three phases illustrate, in the first instance, that a 'technological uncanny' waxes and wanes, but also that the cinema as an institution varies in relation to its surrounding ideologies and modes of address. As it evolved into its second phase of everyday entertainment and modernity, fiction turned the cinema towards other psychic structures, for instance the mechanisms of suspended disbelief that Christian Metz identified with fetishism or the discourses of sexuality and visual pleasure analysed by feminist film theory. This was the cinema that (like the twentieth century itself) left behind the morbid spirit of the Victorians to become an emblem of modernity, both as popular entertainment and as modernist avant-garde. Of course, both these aspects of film culture could and did, in their different ways, recycle the traditions of the uncanny, but for most of the century the cinema's stand was on the side of the new. There is an irony in the way the phantoms conjured up by early cinema have caught up with the ever-increasing crowd of ghosts that now haunt it.

In his essay of 1919, 'The Uncanny', Freud distinguishes between two affects associated with the problem of death. First of all, there is a dread that the already dead might return to haunt the present from the past. Then there is the difficulty for the living subject, while accepting the inevitable, to imagine its own death at some unknown point in the future. While Freud felt that the first, belief in ghosts, could be dismissed as a residue of superstition in the post-Enlightenment world, he thought that the second posed a problem for even the most enlightened minds. In certain circumstances, one fear could summon up the other, perpetuating the power of the irrational over the rational; religious insistence on the existence of an afterlife could feed into belief in the return of the dead. The threshold between life and death becomes a space of uncertainty in which boundaries blur between the rational and the supernatural, the animate and the inanimate. But there is a further opposition between the old and the new that runs through Freud's essay of 1919. For Freud, an uncanny effect can only be produced by the old and he discounts the possibility that the new might make the human mind, and its body, shudder involuntarily.

Freud is, in the first instance, taking issue with Wilhelm Jentsch's essay of 1906, 'On the Psychology of the Uncanny'. He dismisses Jentsch's interest in an uncanny effect that is aroused by the new and the unfamiliar, by automata or waxworks, for instance. And after quite a long detour, he reflects rather on the uncanny nature of death itself, the living body's passage to an inanimate state. However, Freud's uncanny and Jentsch's uncanny come more closely together whenever the animate and the inanimate become confused. A mechanical replica of the human body and the human body from which life has departed both threaten the crucial division between animate and inanimate, organic and inorganic bodies. In one case, the organic body has become inanimate, in the other the inorganic body takes on the appearance of animation. Both are persistent objects of human fear and fascination. In nineteenth-century Paris, for instance, people flocked to see the corpses that were displayed at the Paris morgue as public spectacle. At the same time, they also flocked to see the lifelike waxworks exhibited at the Musée Grévin.[3] However, both Jentsch and Freud note a third phenomenon. Beyond the physical presence of the inanimate body are those narratives in which the dead return to the world of the living as a ghostly apparition: inorganic but animate.

Jentsch, it seems, was interested in the kind of *trompe-l'œil* phenomena that had proliferated with the rise of nineteenth-century optical entertainment and mechanical toys:

> The unpleasant impression is well known that readily arises in many people when they visit collections of wax figures, panopticons and panoramas. In the semi-darkness it is often especially difficult to distinguish a life-size wax or similar figure from a human person . . . whether it is animate or not.

He goes on to say:

> This peculiar effect makes its appearance even more clearly when imitations of the human form not only reach one's perception, but when on top of everything else they appear to be united with certain bodily or mental functions . . . For example, life-size automata that perform complicated tasks, blow trumpets, dance and so forth very easily give one a feeling of unease. The finer the mechanism and the truer to nature the formal reproduction, the more strongly will the special effect also make its appearance.[4]

And he associates the 'uncanny effect' with doubts, 'intellectual uncertainty' about whether 'an apparently animate being is really alive or, conversely, whether a lifeless object might not in fact be animate'.[5] Jentsch's subsequent citation of the E.T.A. Hoffmann stories of automata provokes Freud's rather convoluted digression in 'The Uncanny'. He argues in particular that Olympia, the beautiful mechanical doll in 'The Sandman', is irrelevant to the uncanny aspects of the story, and that the source of the hero's breakdown lies in castration anxiety. ('The Sandman' is discussed further at the end of this chapter.) It is here that Freud asserts his crucial theoretical principle: 'only that class of frightening that leads back to the old and familiar' can be of interest to psychoanalysis. To put it another way, for an emotional effect to have a relation to the unconscious mind, it must have undergone a process of repression from which it may return. The modern and the newfangled could only represent a return of the repressed if they triggered 'something which is familiar and old established in the mind', a formative structure of the unconscious itself, such as the castration complex. It seems that even in 1906 Jentsch was unaware of the cinema's relevance to his proposition. But his comments on replicas of the human body, automata and so on clearly confirmed Freud's theoretical resistance to the new, and to the modern world and its manifestations more generally.

In keeping with his theoretical position, Freud discusses one aspect of the uncanny that is truly archaic, not in the history of the individual psyche, but in the history of human culture. He comments on: 'the uncanny experience ... when primitive beliefs which have been surmounted seem once more to be confirmed'. He identifies the persistence of superstition most closely with the feeling experienced by many people 'in relation to death and dead bodies, to the return of the dead and to spirits and ghosts'. And he points to the near-universal insistence, both by religions and by civil governments, on the existence of life after death:

> There is scarcely any other matter, however, upon which our thoughts and feelings have changed so little since the earliest times,

in which discarded forms have been so completely preserved under
a thin disguise, as our relation to death.[6]

Having dismissed Jentsch's association between the uncanny
and intellectual uncertainty in relation to 'whether an inanimate
object becomes too like an animate one', Freud backtracks slightly:
'And are we after all justified in entirely ignoring intellectual uncertainty as a factor [in the uncanny] seeing that we have admitted its
importance in relation to death?' There are two slightly different
points here. First of all, Freud is referring, somewhat ironically, to
the persistent belief, on the part of 'civilized' people and their religions, in the afterlife and, ultimately, the resurrection of the body.
Secondly, against the precepts of established religion, residues of
archaic fears and superstitions survive: first, the belief that the spirits of the dead are able to visit the living and then that the natural
world is itself inhabited and animated by the presence of spirits.

When he accepts that intellectual uncertainty may be 'a factor',
particularly due to its relation to death, Freud quite incidentally
suggests a way in which his identification of the uncanny with the
'old' may combine with Jentsch's new, mechanical, uncanny.
Uncertainty is a bridging concept linking the two. The popular
cultures of the uncanny had, for quite some time, created illusions
out of uncertainties particular to the human mind, juxtaposing an
uncanny of optical devices and illusions with appearances of
ghosts and the spirits of the dead. In his book *The Great Art of
Light and Shadow*, Laurent Mannoni vividly traces the recurring
association between the magic lantern, and its Gothic offspring,
the phantasmagoria, and the culture of the uncanny. Raising spirits
was the central tour de force of the famous illusions created by
Philidor in the Paris of the Enlightenment and later by Etienne-
Gaspard Robertson after the Revolution. Both claimed that their
performances aimed to 'destroy absurd beliefs, the childish ter-
rors, which dishonour the intelligence of man', but, in its actuality,
the spectacle itself 'sought more to create fear than to dispel the
occult source of fear'. A contemporary commentator described the
effect in the following terms:

Reason has told you well that these are mere phantoms, catoptric tricks devised with artistry, carried out with skill and presented with intelligence, your weakened brain can only believe what it is made to see, and we believe ourselves transported into another world and other centuries.[7]

Tom Gunning, in his introduction to Mannoni's book, draws attention to Freud's concept of the uncanny as the lingering of an irrational belief, often unconscious, after the conscious has dismissed the old belief as nonsense. He then sums up, with great precision, the complex mental processes involved:

As the magic lantern had embodied the marvels of the new science in the seventeenth century, so at the close of the eighteenth it acted out the contest between superstition and reason, with a form of illusion which could invoke both simultaneously. The attraction of the phantasmagoria, which soon became a world-wide form of entertainment, literally enacted the new consciousness of modernity: torn between doubt and credulity, fascinated by the ways its senses could be entertained as its logic sought, not always successfully, for explanations.[8]

This explicit recognition of the space between credulity and knowledge recalls the mid-seventeenth-century Jesuit Athanasius Kircher's insistence that the illusions created by his camera obscura were of nature, not magic. While pointing out that Kircher did not, as is often supposed, invent the magic lantern, Mannoni suggests that he inaugurated a tradition of showmanship that would survive into the magic acts of the nineteenth century:

What Kircher aspired to more than anything was to astonish his followers by the almost universal nature of his knowledge. However, he did not want to pass himself off as a sorcerer, and denounced the quacks who used optics to take advantage of the credulous. Kircher's aim in revealing all these illuminated and shadowy optical tricks was to enlighten the general public.[9]

The concept of uncertainty becomes a nodal point at which disparate ideas meet and branch off in new directions. The masters of phantasmagoria harnessed new technologies to old superstitions, but in the process laid the foundations for something new. The showmen's juggling of contradictions represents a turning point at which they no longer expected their patrons to believe what they saw but to be amazed at the illusions conjured up, distinguishing between the ability to deceive the human eye and to trick the mind. This is an uncertainty of secular materialism that takes pleasure in the culture of illusions and the uncanny and prefigures later forms of mass entertainment. Pleasure in the material relation between illusion and optics and between illusion and momentary credulity, playing with the mind's susceptibility to trickery, all involve various successive phases of exchange between the eye and the mind, belief, doubt, curiosity, that lead towards the uncertainty of Gunning's new consciousness of 'modernity'.

The uncertainty of phantasmagoria also suggests various ways in which Freud's and Jentsch's differing approaches to the inanimate body might be brought into dialogue. First of all, Jentsch's uncanny of 'the new and unfamiliar' leads to the disorientation caused by a 'technological uncanny'. The most rational mind experiences uncertainty when faced with an illusion that is, if only momentarily, inexplicable. As Jentsch puts it: 'even when they know they are being fooled by merely harmless illusions, many people cannot suppress an extremely uncomfortable feeling'.[10] This kind of *frisson* can be located in the moment itself, the sudden moment of doubt, an involuntary and bewildered loss of certainty. A central strand running through the whole history of visual illusions is contained in *this* effect and its investment in *that* moment. It is instantaneous and produced by a particular encounter. Jentsch's argument then meets Freud's uncanny, the persistence in the human mind of belief in the supernatural and the return of the dead. He comments (to repeat the quotation above): 'primitive fear of the dead is still so strong within us and always ready to come to the surface on any provocation'. To bring the two sides together: archaic beliefs and superstitions are able to return within the popular culture of illusions that are not only disorientating but also exploit this particular repressed fear of the dead. As new technologies are often outside popular understanding when they first appear, the most advanced scientific developments can, paradoxically, enable and revive irrational and superstitious beliefs in an animate world. The magic shows the technological uncanny and the magician's illusion merged with a resurrection of the body and the materialization of the spirit world. It is here that Jentsch's interest in the new and the mechanical overlaps with the residues of belief in the supernatural. During the nineteenth century the explosion of new technologies and the popular beliefs that grew up around them overwhelmed the earlier tradition of demystifying the mechanics of illusion and debunking credulity.

According to Tom Gunning, the invention of photography created a new field for enquiry about perception and its relation to knowledge and belief.[11] In particular, the Spiritualist Movement related their revelations to new technologies such as electricity, telegraphy, chemistry and so on. As they first appeared, these technologies seemed paradoxically to give credence to the idea that invisible forces animated the world. The impact that these developments had on the contemporary imagination was not only due to the technological novelties that they produced but also to the fact that they made visible forces that existed, hitherto invisible, within the natural world. A technological novelty gives rise to a technological uncanny, in a collision between science and the supernatural. Thus the intrinsic ghostliness of the black-and-white photograph elided with the sense that the machine might be able to perceive a presence invisible to the human eye. Similarly, the phenomenon of electricity had illustrated the way that the invisible in the natural world could, once harnessed, have powerful visible effects. In their summoning up of ghosts, the Spiritualists exploited on the one hand this new 'animism', the sense of a world filled with spirits at long last made visible; on the other they touched on the longstanding reluctance of the human mind to confront death. Freud comments ironically in his essay 'The Uncanny':

> It is true that the statement 'All Men are Mortal' is paraded in text
> books of logic as an example of a general proposition; but no human
> being really grasps it, and our unconscious has as little use now as it
> ever had for the idea of its own mortality.

And he goes on to mention, also ironically, the renewed fashion for
Spiritualism:

> In our great cities, placards announce lectures that undertake to tell
> us how to get in touch with the souls of the departed; and it cannot
> be denied that not a few of our most able and penetrating minds
> among our men of science have come to the conclusion, especially
> towards the end of their own lives, that a contact of this kind is not
> impossible.[12]

'The Uncanny' was written in 1919, when many of the
bereaved attempted to reach 'the other side' after the appalling loss
of life during World War I. But cultures of and around death were
deeply ingrained in the late nineteenth century. Once the phenomenon of Spiritualism began to move into the realm of show
business and the spectacular, in Gunning's words 'It mined a deep
fascination in visual events that amazed spectators by defying conventional belief.'

Spiritualism and a culture of death, on the one hand, and
rational secularism on the other provided yet another twist to the
space of intellectual and technological uncertainty. The encounter
between 'spectacular spiritualism' and the nineteenth-century
magic show led the showmen to distance themselves from those
charlatans who insisted that their tricks truly raised the dead. John
Neville Maskeleyne, for instance, developed his magic show without, as he put it, the help of spirits. He was a showman who prided
himself on his own skill and ability to make an audience gasp, on
the cusp between credulity and incredulity, 'I don't believe it!'
while seeing with their own eyes. Harry Houdini became deeply

involved in the campaign to debunk Spiritualism, leading to his fraught friendship with Sir Arthur Conan Doyle, who was convinced that he had reached his son, killed in World War I, through a medium. Adam Phillips has described Houdini's implacable hostility to Spiritualism as going beyond professionalism to conviction:

> Like any successful professional magician – and Houdini was the man who put magic on the map, who took it out of quackery and into mainstream entertainment – Houdini had no appetite for the inexplicable; he wasn't keen to be impressed by it. He didn't claim to understand everything, but what had always fascinated him was people's talent for creating mystery. 'Why, Sir Arthur', he once remarked to Doyle, 'I have been trained in mystery all my life and once in a while I see something I can't account for.' But when this happened he wanted to discover how someone had made it. Mystery, for Houdini, was the great secular commodity.[13]

The showmen purged their magic tricks of any connection with the supernatural in order to open up the space for a different kind of amazement. If the audience believed that a divine power had intervened, their emotions would be, indeed, awestruck, but the act would belong to the realm of the supernatural and thus be perfectly explicable. The showmen's aim was to create a space for doubt and generate the *frisson* associated with the breakdown of understanding that gives rise not to a belief in the illusion but to a sense of intellectual uncertainty. This is their modernity. They shifted the cultural agenda towards a kind of super-humanity in which their own transcendent powers were at centre stage. While the rigorous materiality of the performance would cause astonishment, their feats would inevitably raise questions about the limits of the human: how the magicians were able to defy the laws of nature in such a way that an ordinary audience would be unable to decipher what they were seeing.

The invention of photography and its diffusion in the mid-nineteenth century introduced an element of the uncanny that was part of its material process and persisted in its own right after the ghost photographers had disappeared. The uncanny of the phantasmagoria and other ghostly spectacles, in which technology and lingering superstition had been so closely entwined, was recast in rather different terms. The photograph actually preserved, mechanically, a moment of life stopped and then held in perpetuity. It was the extraordinary skill of the showmen both in their technological and artistic preparation and the actual stage management of the show itself that had been the source of their success. While these were beautifully and convincingly conjured illusions, the photograph was the descendant of the 'natural magic' shows of Kircher's and della Porta's camera obscura. It reproduced a record of the real world through the inscription of light, but it was also able to capture and fix that moment of reality on photosensitive material. With photography, the question of time and its passing, its relation to the past, to the 'old' and to death, came into play. Ian Christie has pointed out that uncertainty associated with death was a crucial factor in the late nineteenth-century citizen's response to film:

> What did they want to believe? Essentially that death was not final: that communication with 'the other side' was possible . . . So the respectable Victorians threw themselves into spiritualism, seances, tarot cards and magic of any kinds. In this climate it was scarcely surprising that moving pictures seemed supernatural to their first viewers. Both the Paris papers which reported the first Lumière show ended on the same note: . . . death will cease to be absolute . . . it will be possible to see our nearest alive again long after they have gone.[17]

If the contemporary response to the Lumière films aligns them on side of Freud's ghostly uncanny, Méliès transfers to cinema many characteristic attributes of Jentsch's uncanny, exploiting technological novelty as well as the cinema's ability to blur the boundary between the animate and the inanimate with trick photography. As Paul Hammond describes:

An object can be transformed, either instantaneously or gradually, into another object; an object can grow or diminish before our eyes, while the rest of the image remains a constant size; an object, usually human, can disintegrate into parts, then these can assume a life of their own; an inanimate object can begin to move and an animate one defy the laws of gravity; an object appear or disappear instantaneously or gradually.[15]

And he comments particularly on the phenomenon, noted by Jentsch, whereby inanimate images of the human body take on apparently animate properties:

Not only statues but scarecrows, snowmen, dummies, skeletons. Figures in paintings, posters, photographs, playing card and book illustrations all pulsate with life, through the camera's stop motion capability.[16]

Just as the cinema animated the inanimate photograph, so Méliès used the cinema machine to give life to lifeless representations of the human figure. This aspect of his cinema belongs to a tradition in which replicas of the body acquired the appearance of life, for instance, in the marionette theatre, clockwork toys or the fantastic stories of automata.

Through Jentsch's reference to Olympia, the beautiful automaton in E.T.A. Hoffmann's story 'The Sandman', the question of gender in relation to the uncanny of automata comes to the fore. This is a crucial moment at which Freud takes issue with Jentsch. He argues that the beautiful mechanical doll is irrelevant to the uncanny aspects of the story, and that the source of its hero's breakdown lies in castration anxiety. Olympia introduces the question of gender, if only negatively, into Freud's understanding of the uncanny, into the significance of his opposition between 'old' and 'new' and his dismissive attitude to modernity.

In Hoffmann's story there is indeed ample evidence that its hero, Nathaniel, has had traumatic childhood experiences that could have led to intense castration anxiety. Freud sees his symptoms

Falling in love with Olympia.
From *The Tales of Hoffmann*
(Powell and Pressburger,
UK, 1951).

Olympia dismembered.

very much in terms of displaced anxiety about his eyes provoked
by the two vengeful father figures, the vendor of eye-glasses
Coppola (otherwise known as Coppelius) and Spalanzini, the
'father' of the automaton Olympia. When Coppola sells him a telescope, Nathaniel looks across the street and sees the beautiful and
mysterious young woman in close-up through its lens. It is this
moment that initiates his obsession with Olympia. His previously
normal erotic interest in the scientist's 'beautiful daughter' is transformed into a fetishistic fascination that has materialized out of a
mechanism of enhanced vision, the telescope. The artificial 'cut'

into another space reinforces the displacement that transforms Nathaniel's castration anxiety into disavowal. Olympia is the perfect fetish object. Her wooden, inanimate body is not 'wounded', and she acts as a screen for Nathaniel, reflecting directly back to him his unconscious fantasies, enabling the repression of his fears. Freud's own disavowal of the doll's mediating place in Nathaniel's crisis is so acute that he misreads the tragic ending of the story. Once Nathaniel recovers from the nervous breakdown that had been precipitated by the sight of the two evil father figures fighting over and dismantling Olympia, he is reunited with his living, loving fiancée, Clara. One day, when they climb to the top of a high tower to admire the view, a strange figure in the street below distracts them. Taking out his telescope to look more closely, Nathaniel focuses the lens not, as Freud claims, on Coppola below, but on Clara at his side, whom he mistakes for the wooden doll.[17] His symptoms return and, having tried to throw 'Olympia' from the tower, he falls himself to his death.

Olympia as beautiful automaton also fascinates and horrifies through a technology of vision. She fits well with Annette Michelson's analysis of Hadaly, an exquisite automaton in Villiers de l'Isle Adam's novel *On the Eve of the Future* (first published in Paris in magazine form 1880–81). Michelson argues that the beautiful mechanical woman is, as she puts it, 'the phantasmatical ground of the cinema itself'. Furthermore, the mechanical Hadaly is a figure of transition, which will mutate into the beautiful woman typically featured in the magic shows of Georges Méliès, living but subject to the mechanical tricks of the cinema. This is not woman within cinematic iconography, but the female body 'in an ultimate, phantasmatic mode of representation *as* cinema'.[18] Indeed, there is something about the way that Olympia replaces Clara in Nathaniel's hallucination that suggests a Méliès trick of substitution, one of the key effects in his magic cinema. As he disregards the figure of Olympia, Freud overlooks the crucial place of the female body as fetish and site of displacement for castration anxiety, for which he himself would argue in 1927.[19]

Freud's lack of interest in Olympia, an automaton and apparently a spectacle of the 'technological uncanny', has certain connections to his rejection of the cinema, associated not only with newfangled spectacle but also with the urban culture of the young modern woman. The fashionable flapper (very much the 'new') erased the maternal features (very much, for Freud, the 'old') of the female body, cultivating a boyish flat chest and slim hips. At the same time, her high heels and 'posed' stance evoked a mechanical movement that took femininity away from nature into culture. The flapper had an emblematic relationship to modernity and the robotic world of mechanization. Her heels clicked down the street, her fingers tapped on typewriters and her syncopated high kicks in the chorus line prompted Siegfried Kracauer's well-known comment: 'Technology whose grace is seductive, grace that is genderless because it rests on the joy of precision. A representation of American virtues; a flirt by stopwatch.'[20] Just as the beautiful automaton has no 'inside' apart from her mechanism, these bodies, artificially pre-pubescent, mechanized and modern, are eviscerated. These bodies, Freud might imply, are saved from uncanniness because they repress the womb, and deny the maternal and abject aspects of the woman's body that he sees as a true site of the uncanny:

> It often happens that neurotic men declare that there is something uncanny about the female genital organs. This unheimlich place, however, is the entrance to the former Heim of all human beings, the place where each one of us lived once upon a time and in the beginning.[21]

The mother's body represents the truly ancient for the human psyche. Not only is it the 'first home' itself but its once-upon-a-time memory of security and totality must become abject for the child to become an independent and autonomous being. The automaton in 'The Sandman' could, indeed, lead back, through the process of disavowal, to the ancient problem of the maternal body. An eviscerated, mechanized, femininity masks and marks disavowal of both the site of castration anxiety and the womb, the 'first home'. The element of uncertainty emanates not only from the blurred distinction between the inorganic and the organic but also from the uncertain nature of femininity itself.

Stephen Heath, in his article 'Cinema and Psychoanalysis', has pointed out that Freud's hostility to the cinema is expressed in terms of gender, going beyond his reasonable doubt about its ability to express the complexities of psychoanalytic theory. When refusing, in 1925, to collaborate with Hans Sachs on the development of the film that would be G. W. Pabst's *Secrets of a Soul*, Freud uses telling terms. He says: 'There can be no avoiding the film, any more than one can avoid the fashion for bobbed hair [*Bubikopf*]; I however will not let my hair be cut and will personally have nothing to do with this film.' Heath goes on to point out that Freud's fears of feminization were realized in the image on the *Secrets of a Soul* publicity brochure: 'The gender-anxious, emasculating image is more than appropriate: the cover of Sachs' pamphlet shows the oval of a woman's face … What *does* she want and what does cinema want with psychoanalysis through her and with her for its figure?'[22] For Freud, the cinema was as ephemeral as fashion and, furthermore, through various links between the two, feminine. Indeed, at the time, the cinema was widely understood to be catering to the tastes of the young modern woman. Even Kracauer, for instance, in 1927 titled a series of articles denouncing the politics, aesthetics and ideologies of contemporary popular cinema: 'Little Shop Girls go to the Movies'. From the perspective of the Freudian unconscious, the very modernity of the cinema rendered it uninteresting, celebrating, as it did, with the newest technology, the novelty, speed and glamour of urban life and the robotic, androgynous body of the young modern woman. But these links between femininity, modernity and the cinema suggest that Freud's resistance to the 'new' might lead back through the 'new' to the 'old'.

By the time that Freud associated the cinema with the fashionable and the feminine, it had discarded its association with the cultures of the late nineteenth century. Growing up into the youthfulness of modernity, the cinema acquired its defining attribute: an objective alliance with fiction, stars and glamour. Now, it has aged. Now the cinema seems closer to Freud's uncanny of the old and familiar, and thus, metaphorically, to the archaic body of the mother. Fiction, stars and glamour have undergone a sea change. Those young modern women, who were so anathema to Freud, on film, are unchanged by time. And while they still move with the same mechanical exactitude, acting out the uncanniness of Jentsch's automata, they belong to a world that has been relegated to the distant past by time and in cinema to its history. To look back into the reality of that lost world by means of the cinema is to have the sensation of looking into a time machine. However clichéd the concept, the presence of that reality, of the past preserved, becomes increasingly magical and uncanny. Furthermore, as electronic and digital technologies have overtaken the cinema and, as a new 'new' arrives, the old 'new' becomes relegated to 'the old'. Paradoxically and incidentally, the new technologies have contributed further to bringing the uncanny back to the cinema. The ease with which the moving image can now be halted exposes the cinema's mechanisms and the illusion of its movement, as though the beautiful automaton had become stuck in a particular pose.

Film historians have pointed out, quite correctly, that the cinema and its prehistory are too deeply imbricated, ideologically and technologically, for an abrupt 'birth of the cinema' to be conceptually valid. But from the perspective of the uncanny, the arrival of celluloid moving pictures constitutes a decisive moment. It was only then that the reality of photography fused with mechanical movement, hitherto restricted to animated pictures, to reproduce the illusion of life itself that is essential to the cinema. But the image of life was necessarily haunted by deception. In the cinema organic movement is transformed into its inorganic replica, a series of static, inanimate, images, which, once projected, then become animated to blur the distinctions between the oppositions. The homologies extend: on the one hand, the inanimate, inorganic, still, dead; on the other, organic, animate, moving, alive. It is here, with the blurring of these boundaries, that the uncanny nature of the cinematic image returns most forcefully and, with it, the conceptual space of uncertainty: that is, the difficulty of understanding time and the presence of death in life. We can certainly say, with Freud, that we have 'surmounted' belief in the return of the dead, of animate forces in nature and even belief in the afterlife. However, the presence of the past in the cinema is also the presence of the body resurrected and these images can trigger, if only by association, questions that still seem imponderable: the nature of time, the fragility of human life and the boundary between life and death.

Chapter Three
The Index and the Uncanny:
Life and Death in the Photograph

Standing, as Rosalind Krauss puts it, rather strangely at the crossroads of science and the spiritualism, still photography had already, immediately after its invention, generated associations with life after death, while also supplying, for the first time in human history, a mechanized imprint of reality.[1] This 'crossroads' also marks a point where an indexical sign of Peircian semiotic theory overlaps with an uncanny of Freudian psychoanalytic theory. Both André Bazin, in 'The Ontology of the Photographic Image', first published in 1945, and Roland Barthes, in *Camera Lucida*, first published in 1970, discuss this apparent contradiction, although in different ways. Bazin was writing, implicitly, about the cinema; Barthes was writing explicitly not about the cinema. Colin MacCabe has pointed out that Barthes's reflections on photography in *Camera Lucida* are strikingly close to, but fail to acknowledge, the 'Ontology' article. He attributes this oversight to the way that Bazin, although always of continuing importance to film theorists, underwent a certain intellectual eclipse in the era of structuralism and semiotics so closely associated with Barthes. As MacCabe puts it, 'His Catholic humanism and realist aesthetic had banished him from the theoretical reading lists of the '60s and '70s.'[2] This precise mixture, the religious and the realist, drew Bazin to Rossellini and also formed the backdrop to his thoughts on the photograph. In *Camera Lucida*, questions of religion, magic and the supernatural do figure, more surprisingly, alongside an uncompromising insistence on the index. These points of coincidence between the two derive not only from intellectual and aesthetic analysis but also from a common, almost bewildered, fascination with the photograph as a phenomenon that goes beyond the intellectual and the aesthetic. The index, an incontrovertible fact, a material trace that can be left without human intervention, is a property of the camera machine and the chemical impact of light on film. A sense of the uncanny, often experienced as a collapse of rationality, is a property of the human mind and its uncertainties. A re-reading of Barthes and Bazin on photography reveals ways in which the two, the index and the uncanny, interweave in their reflections on both sides of this contradiction.

Peter Wollen, in his pioneering application of C. S. Peirce's semiotic to photography and cinema, points out that Peirce himself made the link between physical presence and physical inscription:

> Photographs, especially instantaneous photographs, are very instructive, because we know that in certain respects they are exactly like the objects they represent. But this resemblance is due to the photographs having been produced under such circumstances that they were physically forced to correspond point by point to nature. In that aspect then, they belong to the second class of signs, those by physical connection.[3]

An emphasis on the index, on the 'physical connection', and on the trace and its inscription, lies at the heart of Roland Barthes's *Camera Lucida*. He describes the photographic process as:

> the printing of luminous rays emitted by an object on photosensitive material. Thus, in spite of all possible human interference, it is this characteristic that differentiates photography from other forms of representation . . . It is as if the photograph always carries the referent within itself.[4]

Without using the semiotic terminology of *Camera Lucida*, André Bazin also sees the photograph as index and his interest is close to Barthes's:

The photograph as such and the object itself share a common being, after the fashion of a finger print. Wherefore, photography actually contributes something to the order of natural creation instead of substituting for it.[5]

For both Bazin and Barthes, the photograph's beauty and emotional appeal lies in its 'thereness', the fleeting presence of a shadow, which is captured and saved. Bazin says:

The photographic image is the object itself. The object freed from the conditions of time and space which govern it . . . [the photographic image] shares, by virtue of the very process of becoming, the being of the model of which it is the reproduction: it is the model.

Photographs made, for instance, by placing objects on photosensitive paper and exposing them to light vividly exemplify the 'process of becoming' that is only more mechanically complex with light focused through a camera lens.

The index, fixed as it is in the photograph, is a record of a fraction of time. When rays of light record an object's presence they also inscribe that moment of time, henceforth suspended. Although, once again, Bazin does not, in so many words, draw specific attention to the temporality of the photograph, its importance recurs implicitly throughout the 'Ontology' essay and specifically as a characteristic of the index:

Hence the charm of family albums. Those gray or sepia shadows, phantomlike and almost indecipherable, are no longer traditional family portraits but rather the disturbing presence of lives halted at a set moment in their duration, freed from their destiny; not however by the prestige of art but by the power of an impassive mechanical process: for photography does not create eternity as art does, it embalms time, rescuing it simply from its own proper corruption.[6]

Once time is 'embalmed' in the photograph, it persists, carrying the past across to innumerable futures as they become the present.

This persistence characterizes the embalmed index whatever it might be. But because the photograph captures the presence of life stilled, the instantaneous nature of human movement and the fragility of human life, it confuses time more thoroughly than, for instance, the presence of a ruin or a landscape in which traces of the past are preserved. Out of this link between a past moment and the future, Barthes translates the photograph's relation to time into tense. For him, the photographic image is a recording of absence and presence simultaneously:

> What I see has been here, in this place which extends between infinity and the subject (operator or spectator); it has been here and immediately separated; it has been absolutely irrefutably present, and yet already deferred.[7]

In order to articulate this strange sense of displacement, Barthes makes use of 'shifters', terms of spatial position, 'here' and 'there', demonstrative pronouns, 'this' and 'that', and, at other times, terms of temporal position, 'now' and 'then'. He points out that a photograph's journey through time forces its viewer to find words to articulate the difficulty of expressing its uncertain temporality. And he has recourse to shifter terminology in the process of trying to pin down the coexistence of 'now' and 'then'. He combines the materiality and flexibility of the shifter with tense: 'then' the photograph was 'there' at its moment of registration, 'that' moment is now 'here'. He sums up photography's essence as 'this was now'.

Writing about *Camera Lucida*, Ann Banfield suggests that Barthes's use of the shifter, or deixis, marks a point at which language may simply not be adequate to describe the photograph's tense:

> Like Proust, Barthes' effort is to find the linguistic form capable of recapturing a present in the past, a form that it turns out spoken language does not offer. This now-in-the-past can be captured not by combining tenses but by combining a past tense with a present time deictic: the photograph's moment *was now*.[8]

She draws on novelistic tense structure to argue that the 'was', needed to imply 'a now-in-the-past', would become: 'This was now here'. These markers of time and place return to Barthes's original conundrum. She says: '"This was now here" stands for "an emanation of past reality"'.[9] The photograph pushes language and its ability to articulate time to the limits of its possibility, leaving the spectator with a slightly giddy feeling, reminiscent of the effect caused by *trompe-l'œil*. But since this is an oscillation of time rather than of space, it is even more abstract and difficult to articulate, and gives rise to that sense of uncertainty associated with the uncanny.

The human imagination engages with the mechanical integrity of photographic registration, its place on the side of the index, its indiscriminate recording of everything in front of the lens, leaving on one side the photographer's intervention and organization. It is the mechanical and indexical nature of the image that leads to the slippage of language demanded by a past that persists into the present. Barthes's use of words acknowledges this and recalls his citation, early in *Camera Lucida*, of Jacques Lacan's concept of the Real, the aspect of human experience that stands outside the grasp of language. The photograph, however influenced it might be by its surrounding culture or its maker's vision, is affected by the Real both in its materiality and in the human subject's response to it. There is the difficulty of conceptualizing fully the inhuman nature of the camera machine and its ability to hold time, but there is also the resonance of death that culture and the human imagination have associated with photographic images. From this perspective, the slippage of language is a symptom of the presence of death and its inevitability.

In the 'Ontology' essay, Bazin begins by identifying the origin of art, of the making of a likeness, as driven by the human desire to overcome death. Then he identifies the death mask as the origin of images made from a direct imprint, tracing the practice back to the 'mummification' of bodies in ancient Egypt. The death mask is, of course, an index; it is an image formed by an actual imprint of the deceased's features. Bazin says: 'Death is but the victory of time.

To preserve the bodily appearance artificially is to snatch it from the flow of time, to stow it neatly away, so to speak, in the hold of life.'[10] This process, holding the flow of time, or 'embalming' time, and preserving the actual features of the dead person through an imprinted image, would, Bazin argues, be realized finally and perfectly with photography. Photography would thus take over a function that art had struggled, in the meantime, to fulfill. This sweeping history of art, its relation to death and to photography, takes up only a few paragraphs of the 'Ontology' essay. But the connection was understood very quickly in the nineteenth century as people adopted photography into the rituals of mourning and memorials. The deathbed photograph came to replace the death mask. Both record the reality of the dead body and, in preserving it, assume a ghostly quality.

In *Camera Lucida*, the presence of death in the photograph is a constantly recurring and pervasive theme throughout the book, approached from various different angles. But at one point Barthes makes a rare move to comment on the history of photography, reflecting on the coincidence of its origins with the decline of religion and suggesting that, with photography, death is inscribed into life without the mediation of religion or ritual:

All those young photographers who are at work in the world, determined upon the capture of actuality, do not know that they are agents in the capture of death . . . for my part I should prefer that instead of constantly relocating the advent of photography in its social and economic context, we should inquire as to the anthropological place of death and the new image. For death must be somewhere in a society; if it is no longer (or less intensely) in religion it must be elsewhere; perhaps in this image which produces death while trying to preserve life. Contemporary with the withdrawal of rites, Photography may respond to the intrusion, in our modern society, of an asymbolic death, outside of religion, outside of ritual, a kind of abrupt dive into literal death. Life / Death; the paradigm is reduced to a single click, the one separating the initial pose from the final print.[11]

Camera Lucida gradually reveals its emotional core. Barthes uses his mourning for his recently deceased mother as the context for his reflections on photography. The themes of time, of the photograph and then of death come more clearly to the surface and are more closely woven together. Not only is the essence of photography, the 'this was now', subject to the passing of time within the course of a life, but it then becomes, in Barthes's words: 'That rather terrible thing that is there in every photograph: the return of the dead.'

In the first instance, for Bazin and Barthes, photography touches the complex human relation to death, but their shared perspective then diverges. For Bazin, it is to transcend death, part of the process of mourning; for Barthes, it is 'the dive into death', an acceptance of mortality. Barthes's intensely personal engagement with the photograph is a response to his mother's recent death but also extends to his own future death. His journey into photography is reminiscent of Freud's remark (in a very different context) 'Si vis vitam, para mortem. If you want to endure life, prepare yourself for death.'[12] If his reflections on the photograph enable Barthes to encounter his own mortality, Bazin, as a Catholic, would, needless to say, have believed in a life after death, by which '[death] is snatched away from the hold of time' into everlasting life.

The photograph's early associations with death and the supernatural were given a particular inflection by its arrival in a culture in which death and mourning played a prominent part, accentuated by the promises of religion and many a bereaved person's hopes of making contact with 'the other side'.[13] These are the kind of beliefs that Freud refers to in his essay of 1919, 'The Uncanny'. While assuming that they would have less and less hold after the Enlightenment, he also points out how easily the rationality of 'civilization' may be jolted by some phenomenon that suggests supernatural intervention in the natural world. Uncanny feelings are aroused by confusion between the animate and the inanimate, most particularly again associated with death and the return of the dead. The photograph's suspension of time, its conflation of life and death, the animate and the inanimate, raises not superstition so much as a sense of disquiet that is aggravated rather than calmed by the photograph's mechanical, chemical and indifferent nature. Jacques Derrida, commenting on Barthes's association between photography and death, emphasizes the dominance of the mechanical, as he puts it, of *techne*, which leaves little or no room in photography for human intervention in the form of art:

> Whatever the nature of the art of photography, that is to say, its inter-
> vention, its style, there is a point at which the photographic act is not
> an artistic act, a point at which it registers passively and this poignant,
> piercing passivity represents the opportunity of this reference to
> death; it seizes a reality that is there, that was there in an indissoluble
> now. In a word, one must choose between art and death.[14]

Barthes's concept of the *punctum* is also based on a separation between the eye of the photographer and the eye of the camera. A detail, probably unnoticed by the photographer, suddenly captures the viewer's attention and emotion. The detail is poignant precisely because its presence is a mark of the camera's indifference, its inability to discriminate between its subject and the subject's surrounding. Walter Benjamin also comments on the significance of chance in his 'Short History of Photography':

> However skilful the photographer, however carefully he poses his
> model, the spectator feels an irresistible compulsion to look for the
> tiny spark of chance, of the here and now, with which reality has, as
> it were, seared the character in the picture; to find that imperceptible
> point at which, in the immediacy of that long-past moment, the
> future so persuasively inserts itself, that, looking back we may redis-
> cover it.[15]

Here, too, the relation is between the instant photographed and the delayed viewer, between the camera's time and its address to the future. Barthes's *punctum* similarly provokes a sudden and involuntary emotional response, differentiating it from the *studium*, the term he uses to describe the presence of social, cultural or other meanings that have been consciously invested in the image. The *studium* belongs to the photographer; the *punctum* to the viewer.

Barthes also associates the photograph's *punctum* with a sudden and overwhelming consciousness of death:

> In 1865, young Lewis Payne attempted to assassinate Secretary of State W. H. Seward. Alexander Gardner photographed him in his cell where he was waiting to be hanged. The photograph is handsome, as is the boy: that is the *studium*. But the *punctum* is: *he is going to die*. I read at the same time: *This will be* and *this has been*; I observe with horror an anterior future of which death is the stake . . . In front of the photograph of my mother as a child, I tell myself: she is going to die: I shudder, like Winnicott's psychotic patient, *over a catastrophe that has already occurred*. Whether or not the subject is already dead, every photograph is this catastrophe.[16]

He sums up this aspect of the *punctum* as 'this vertigo of time defeated'. Beyond the question of death, an overwhelming and irrational sense of fate or destiny, of an outside intervention in the everyday, is also a mark of the uncanny. Such a disordering of the sensible in the face of sudden disorientation is similar to *déjà vu*, involuntary memory, a suddenly half-remembered dream or the strange sense of reality breaking through the defences of the conscious mind. These are all mental phenomena that overwhelm consciousness and they happen, as Barthes says, 'in a floating flash', producing a sense of uncertainty that may be pleasurable or frightening. Freud describes the uncanny as a moment when 'the distinction between imagination and reality is suddenly effaced'. And, finally: 'Are we after all justified in entirely ignoring intellectual uncertainty as a factor seeing that we have admitted its importance in relation to death?'[17]

Both Bazin and Barthes dwell on the fact that the photograph is 'not made by the hand of man' and is 'a mechanical reproduction in the making of which man plays no part'. In her discussion of *Camera Lucida*, Ann Banfield elaborates on Barthes's idea that the camera records more than the photographer can ever hope to see. At the moment when the lens is opened, its eye takes over from the photographer's eye: 'This sight is a sight reduced to the simply seen, from whose subjective image – the this-was now here – all subjectivity that requires a subject, an I, is eliminated.'[18]

> . . . that subject's continued existence, along with anything that he or she may have thought or felt about the sensation, becomes superfluous, unnecessary the instant the shutter is released; the image separates itself irrevocably from those simultaneous thoughts to assume as separate unthinking existence.[19]

Just as the photograph's relation to time goes beyond equivalence in the grammar of tense, so the autonomy of the camera eye goes beyond the grammar of person. The human factor is displaced.

If the photograph marks a meeting point between a material, physical document and a twinge of uncertainty in rationality, two factors come particularly into play. First of all there is the 'intellectual uncertainty' associated with death and the uncanny contained in the human imagination's engagement with the photograph. Secondly, there is the 'intellectual impossibility' of reducing the photograph to language and a grammatical system of meaning, the presence of an intractable reality in the index. Throughout both Bazin's and Barthes's essays, expressions of paradox and ambivalence recur, bearing witness to the surprising connection between reality and the uncanny. Both writers evoke a narrow, or blurred, boundary between emanations of the material world and those of the human imagination. Although Bazin's main area of interest and passion was the cinema, the 'Ontology' article reveals, crucially and explicitly, the foundation of his aesthetic on the photographic index. But there is a connection between the importance of the index for Bazin's aesthetics and his Catholic belief in the place of God in nature and the human soul. Peter Wollen says:

> Realism, for Bazin, had little to do with mimesis . . . It was the existential bond between fact and image, world and film, which counted

for most in Bazin's aesthetic, rather than any quality of similarity or resemblance. Hence the possibility – even the necessity – of an art which could reveal spiritual states. There was, for Bazin, a double movement of impression, moulding and imprinting: first the interior spiritual suffering was stamped upon the exterior physiognomy; then the exterior physiognomy was stamped and printed on the sensitive film.[20]

It is possible to imagine that Barthes had Bazin in mind when he made this commitment of principle:

> Nothing can prevent the Photograph from being analogical; but at the same time, Photography's *noeme* has nothing to do with analogy (a feature it shares with all kinds of representations). The realists, of whom I am one . . . do not take the photograph for a 'copy' of reality, but for an emanation of past reality: a magic not an art.[21]

For Bazin, the photograph is 'an image that is a reality of nature, namely an hallucination that is also a fact'. His use of language indicates the way in which, for him, the photograph as index almost literally 'haunts' the blurred boundary between life and death. He uses words and terms that evoke the ghostly, for instance: 'the shadows, phantom like . . . the disturbing presence of lives halted . . . the mechanical process, which embalms time against corruption'. Barthes describes his persistent astonishment at the photograph that:

> reaches down into the religious substance of which I am moulded; nothing for it: photography has something to do with resurrection: might we not say of it, as the Byzantines said of the image of Christ which impregnated St Veronica's napkin: that it was not made by the hand of man, achieropoitos.[22]

In the complex and personal development of his ideas in *Camera Lucida*, Barthes moves from the material (the photograph as index, its inscription in and of time) to the immaterial (the photographic image as a 'return of the dead', the hallucination) to a resonance between photography and religion itself. In the process, he takes his argument from the photograph as the material trace of the natural to the photograph as the site of 'intellectual uncertainty'. That is, from a usual association between the photograph and its 'being there', its assertion of a once-upon-a-time moment that existed in the world, to human perplexity in the face of death, which tends to be drawn towards irrationality and the need to believe.

It is the photograph as index, located as it is in an 'embalmed' moment, that enables these exchanges across the boundaries between the material and the spiritual, reality and magic, and between life and death. Its most material aspect, the physical, 'existential', link between object and image, gives rise to the most elusive and ineffable properties of this particular sign. The photographic index, the most literal, the most banal of signs, is inscribed into the clouded, occluded, terrain in which even Freud allows that intellectual uncertainty persists within the frame of 'civilization'. This contradiction was central to Rossellini, poised as he was between Bazin's Catholicism and Barthes's dive into death, also a realist and a believer in magic. In the same spirit Benjamin comments that the difference between technology and magic is 'entirely a matter of historical variables'.[23]

Ann Banfield cites Barthes: 'Something in the image, as revealed by the photograph, leads one "to confront in it the wakening of intractable reality"'.[24] At the very beginning of *Camera Lucida*, Barthes cites Lacan's term the *tuche* to evoke 'the This . . . the Real in its indefatigable expression'.[25] The concept of an 'intractable reality' leads back to Freud's theory of trauma as an event or experience that arouses too much psychic excitement for the subject to be able to translate its significance into words. Trauma leaves a mark on the unconscious, a kind of index of the psyche that parallels the photograph's trace of an original event. This analogy became more telling as photography expanded into news reporting, developing, during the twentieth century, into a record of disaster and death that covered similar ground to that of Goya. This literal link between trauma and the photograph enabled an element of the unspeakable, Lacan's Real, to find a place within the still uncertain and unstable discourses of history and memory. Although the Real cannot be grasped or dealt with directly, these photographic images reach out, making a gesture towards the political and social aspects of traumatic experience.

For Barthes the cinema's relentless movement, reinforced by the masquerade and movement of fiction, could not offer the psychic engagement and emotion he derived from the still photograph. Unlike the photograph, a movie watched in the correct conditions (24 frames a second, darkness) tends to be elusive. Like running water, fire or the movement of trees in the wind, this elusiveness has been intrinsic to the cinema's fascination and its beauty. The insubstantial and irretrievable passing of the celluloid film image is in direct contrast to the way that the photograph's stillness allows time for the presence of time to emerge within the image. New moving image technologies, the electronic and the digital, paradoxically allow an easy return to the hidden stillness of the film frame. This stillness is, of course, an illusion. It is not the actual frame, as stilled for the twenty-fourth of a second in front of the lens; it is not the chemically produced image of celluloid. But the frozen frame restores to the moving image the heavy presence of passing time and of the mortality that Bazin and Barthes associate with the still photograph.

Chapter Four
The Death Drive:
Narrative Movement Stilled

The cinema is divided into two parts, linked by a beam of light, split between its material substance, the unglamorous celluloid strip running through the projector on one side and, on the other, entrancing images moving on a screen in a darkened space. By and large, most film, especially fiction, has struggled for an independent identity, as though its images were born fully matured in movement on the screen. The avant-garde has, on the contrary, consistently brought the mechanism and the material of film into visibility, closing the gap between the filmstrip and the screen. This division, however, goes beyond a simple question of material, its exposure or repression, and revolves around the fundamental, and irreconcilable, opposition between stillness and movement that reverberates across the aesthetics of cinema. Stillness and movement have different relations to time. The illusion of movement is necessarily extended within time, in duration. A still frame when repeated creates an illusion of stillness, a freeze frame, a halt in time. Stillness may evoke a 'before' for the moving image as filmstrip, as a reference back to photography or to its own original moment of registration. Although the projector reconciles the opposition and the still frames come to life, this underlying stillness provides cinema with a secret, with a hidden past that might or might not find its way to the surface. The inanimate frames come to life, the unglamorous mechanics are covered over and the entrancing illusion fills the screen. But like the beautiful automaton, a residual trace of stillness, or the hint of stillness within movement, survives, sometimes enhancing, sometimes threatening.

The avant-garde cinema that has given particular attention to the filmstrip and its frames, working very precisely with the divided cinema, is the flicker film. Peter Kubelka, for instance, has described his films in the following way:

> People always feel that my films are very even and have no edges and do not break apart and are equally heavy at the beginning and the end. This is because the harmony spreads out of the unit of the frame, of the one twenty fourth of a second, and I depart from this ground rhythm, from twenty-four frames, which you feel, you always feel. Even when you see a film by de Mille, you feel it prrrrr as it goes on the screen.[1]

Kubelka's films are built around a 'metric rhythm' creating a film time from the celluloid strip, a succession of still frames that file past the projector beam, the primary source of light. Thierry Kuntzel's concept of *défilement* refers to those films of moving figures filing past the camera that appear so often in early cinema. This, too, is a distilled movement in which the succession of people almost seems to emerge from a succession of frames, echoing the projector's movement.[2] In the Lumière brothers' film *A Boat Leaving the Harbour* the waves and the rowers' actions combine to build up, in Kubelka's words, 'this ground rhythm' or, in Kuntzel's, *défilement*. Across the history of the cinema, obviously to varying degrees, cars, trains or other vehicles have realized the movement of the cinema machine, the projector's rhythmic 'prrrr', slightly detached from the surrounding scene and slightly attached to the mechanism of cinema. But in spite of these residual 'memories' of stillness within movement, the relation between the aesthetics of cinema and mobility is transcended by the camera, by editing and ultimately by narrative, all of which tend to disguise the other side of the divide.

Lynne Kirby, writing about the significance of the railway for early cinema, points out:

> [The train] is a metaphor in the Greek sense of the word: move-
> ment, the conveyance of meaning. Like the film's illusion of
> movement the experience of the railroad is a fundamental paradox:
> simultaneous motion and stillness.[3]

The affinity between the two machines is supplemented by a visual
representation of mechanical movement. From the stillness and
movement of frame and projector in the flicker film, in which the
actual 'paradox' appears on the screen, the affinity is realized in
visual equivalents that translate and extend the movement of the
camera. In the opposition between stillness and movement and the
division between the projector and the screen, camera movement
gives a further dimension to the illusion created by the filmstrip
moving at 24 frames a second. And then, in addition to crane,
tracking and panning shots, forward movement in actual scenes
accentuates the camera's movement. In his discussion of the
'movement-image' Gilles Deleuze makes this connection:

> What counts is that the mobile camera is like a general equivalent of
> all the means of locomotion that it shows or that it makes use of –
> aeroplane, car, boat, bicycle, foot, metro . . . Wenders was to make
> this equivalence the soul of his two films *Kings of the Road* and *Alice
> in the Cities*, thus introducing into the cinema a particularly con-
> crete reflection on the cinema. In other words, the essence of
> cinematic movement-image lies in extracting from vehicles or mov-
> ing bodies the movement which is their common substance, or
> extracting from movements the mobility which is their essence.[4]

These attributes of cinema's movement dovetail with those of
narrative's form and structure. The most significant entertainment
of twentieth-century popular culture was created by an aesthetic
affinity as well as an objective alliance between the two. Cinema's
forward movement, the successive order of film, merges easily into
the order of narrative. Linearity, causality and the linking figure of
metonymy, all crucial elements in story-telling, find a correspon-
dence in the unfolding, forward-moving direction of film. While

the main, middle, section of narrative is characterized by a drive forward, beginnings and ends are, on the contrary, characterized by stasis. Narrative needs a motor force to start up, out of an inertia to which it returns at the end. The cinematic image can find visual equivalents for these different phases: an initial stillness, then the movement of camera and character carry forward and energize the story, from shots to sequences through the linking process of editing. But at the end, the aesthetics of stillness returns to both narrative and the cinema. Death as a trope that embodies the narrative's stillness, its return to an inanimate form, extends to the cinema, as though the still frame's association with death fuses into the death of the story, as though the beautiful automaton was to wind down into its inanimate, uncanny, form. In this sense, endings present different kind of aesthetic exchange between narrative and cinema. Freud's concept of 'the death drive' negotiates between the two, including, as it does, movement towards an end as the desire to return to an 'earlier' state.

In his essay 'Freud's Master Plot', Peter Brooks has applied Freud's essay 'Beyond the Pleasure Principle' specifically to questions of narrative structure to find parallels between the death drive and the movement of narrative towards a final halt. There are two phases to his argument. He begins by establishing the initial relation between narrative movement and stillness in its psychoanalytic dimension, with desire as the motor force that takes a story out of inertia:

> The description of narrative needs metonymy (the figure of contiguity, combination and the syntagmatic relation), the figure of linkage in the signifying chain: precedence and consequence, the movement from one detail to another, the movement towards totalisation under the mandate of desire.[5]

Brooks, having argued that the momentum and metonymy of desire mesh with the momentum and metonymy of narrative drive, moves on to consider their ultimately contradictory dependence on stasis. If desire activates a story then that same force seeks a means to return, at the end, once more to stasis. Here Brooks turns to Freud's theory of the death drive. According to Freud:

> Conservative instincts are therefore bound to give a deceptive appearance of being forces towards change and progress, whilst in fact they are merely seeking to reach an ancient goal by paths alike old and new . . . it would be a contradiction to the conservative nature of the instincts if the goal of life were a state of things which had never yet been attained. On the contrary, it must be an old state of things, an initial state from which the living entity has at one time or other departed and to which it is striving to return by the circuitous paths along which its development leads.[6]

Throughout 'Beyond the Pleasure Principle', the stimulation to movement, inherent in the death instinct, jostles with its aim to return, to rediscover the stillness from which it originally departed. Freud's metaphors, 'paths' and 'depart' alongside 'return' and 'initial state', resonate with the topographies of narrative structure. These are the elements that allow Brooks to perceive a 'master plot' at work. He argues (paralleling Freud) that narrative's movement also needs to find a way back to 'an earlier state of things' through death: 'The more we inquire into the problem of ends, the more it seems to compel an inquiry into its relation to the human end.'[7]

There are two grand conventions of narrative closure, devices that allow the drive of a story to return to stasis: death or marriage. Marriage as closure also brings with it the topographical stasis conventionally implied by the new home, the 'palace' in which a hero settles, after his travels, balancing the family home from which he had originally departed. Within the conventions of popular cinema, the final, emblematic, kiss very often provides an image for the erotic stasis of marriage in 'The End'. But in this narrative pattern, marriage is usually achieved only once the hero has defeated the villain, whose death is the inevitable companion to a 'happy end'. Both represent a formal limit of narrative and figure its closure. In his analysis of narrative pattern, Brooks draws attention to the part played by death as a figuration of closure in more novelistic, less folkloristic, narratives. Here, narrative 'ending', which brings with it the silence and stillness associated with death, is doubled by the hero's death within the world of the story: 'The more we inquire into the problem of ends, the more it seems to compel an inquiry into its relation to the human end.'

Of all the means of achieving narrative stasis, death has a particular tautological appeal, a doubling of structure and content. Other kinds of story-telling resist this kind of formalism, reaching out beyond an ending to the continued flow of life or with an insistence on movement as opposed to stasis. According to Jacques Rivette:

> For there are films which begin and end, which have a beginning and an ending, which conduct their story from an initial premise until everything has been restored to peace and order, and there have been deaths, a marriage or a revelation; there is Hawks, Hitchcock, Murnau, Ray, Griffith. And there are films quite unlike this, which recede into time like rivers to the sea; and which offer us only the most banal of closing images: rivers flowing, crowds, armies, shadows passing, curtains falling in perpetuity, a girl dancing till the end of time; there is Renoir and Rossellini.[8]

The tropes of stillness and movement that order narrative structure are realized in cinema in literal forms, objects or actions. In Michael Powell and Emeric Pressburger's *The Red Shoes* (1948), for instance, the opening sequence, the transition from narrative's initial inertia, uses the literal rush of the hero's movement into the story as its trigger. But the film starts with an image of stasis, a still shot held for a few seconds on closed doors. Then the story's opening is signalled as the doors open and the screen is overwhelmed by a crowd who carry this first forward movement into a sequence of shots up long flights of stairs. The rhetorical imagery of these shots then gains content. These are music students, racing for the best seats in the gallery at Covent Garden, and their upward movement (towards 'the gods') comes to stand, not so much for their poverty, but rather for their burning artistic ambition. The

The death of the dancer: the end of the ballet in *The Red Shoes* (Powell and Pressburger, 1948).

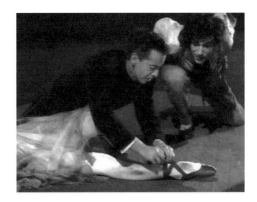

The death of the dancer: the end of the film.

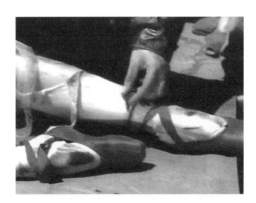

The dance goes on.

film's hero, Julian (Marius Goring), is singled out as he fights for the lead, driven harder by his ambition, the 'desire' in Brooks's terms, which will drive the story. The sequence covers three textual levels. First of all, on a material level: the initial image of the closed doors represents narrative stasis and, implicitly, the stillness of cinema. Then the cinema's movement captures the forward drive of narrative, both embodied by the rushing crowd, as well as the metonymic force of montage as the sequence builds from shot to shot. Julian represents the transformation of this initial movement into the personified desire that will fuel the story. His bodily presence on the screen goes beyond character, interweaving these psychoanalytic, narrative and cinematic strands. 'Body' and 'embodiment' can no longer be distinguished. The image of embodied movement becomes, as it were, a metaphor for the metonymic forward drive of narrative itself. And the images of movement on the screen are brought to life by the filmstrip's forward movement on the projector's reel. The mechanical, prosaic, quality of the projector's start and halt gains an aesthetic reflection in narrative beginnings and endings.

The Red Shoes is about dance. Its heroine, Vicky (Moira Shearer), is, at the beginning of the film, an aspiring ballerina consumed by the desire to dance. She joins Boris Lermontov's (Anton Walbrook) Ballet Company, where her career takes off with her performance of the ballet 'The Red Shoes'. When she marries Julian about two-thirds of the way through the story, he forbids her to dance. After she attempts to return to the ballet, Julian and Lermontov confront her with a choice between marriage and the ballet. The film ends when Vicky jumps to her death in front of the Paris express, her suicide also representing the death of the narrative, its return to stasis. These themes, movement and stillness, dance and death, are central to the ballet of 'The Red Shoes' itself. When the red shoes force the heroine to dance, the cinema takes over from the stage, shifting gradually into a hallucinatory world in which the movement of the cinema merges with the movement of the dance that can only stop with death. But the themes are also spread across the story of the film itself. Trains stand for the ballet company's restless movement on tour. They are the dancers' literal means of transport, but also more figuratively they represent a nomadic, unsettled way of living that is incompatible with marriage. The opposition is prefigured in an early scene, when Lermontov sacks the company's prima ballerina as she announces her engagement. Her parting with the company takes place at the railway station, visually dividing the paths of travel and marriage. The company's movement on tour is repetitive, indicated by the journeys, the succession of trains, cities and labelled luggage. There is also a different kind of repetition in the processes of rehearsal and performance and the discipline of ballet that always returns to the beginning, the practice bar, however great the stage success the night before.

While Freud describes the death drive as the desire to return to an 'old state of things', he also associates it with a compulsion to repeat. Ballet in *The Red Shoes* is depicted as compulsive and all-consuming, revolving around the repeated movements of the dance, with Lermontov's relation to the company representing the will to power and mastery, the sadism that Freud also saw in the death instinct. Although these relations are depicted poignantly rather than sadistically, the shadow of the dominating dancing master, the manipulative puppeteer, hovers over Lermontov, and the narrow edge between the dancer and the automaton is specifically evoked when Vicky dances *Coppelia*. Lermontov is, however, himself caught in the unceasing flow of repetition and return that works to renew rather than to destroy the movement of the ballet. Marriage brings this constant, circling movement and the theme of repetition to a halt and takes place, inappropriately, in the middle section of the story, as a figure of blockage rather than of the happy end. In contrast to the flow and repetition that characterizes the ballet, Julian's desire is linear and it is the erotic in the narrative that is fuelled by the death drive. The story's end in the stasis of death rather than marriage retrospectively illuminates Julian's relation to Vicky as that of Olympia and Nathaniel in reverse. Rather than fetishizing her appearance of life, his desire reduces her to motionlessness, like the run-down automaton. The train, which will be the instrument of Vicky's suicide, approaches Monte Carlo in an apparent symmetry to Julian's first headlong rush up the stairs at Covent Garden, balancing the momentum of the beginning with the oncoming figure of death. In *The Red Shoes* the attributes of the death drive diverge in a separation that is inflected by gender. On the one hand, there is Julian's desire to master both the story and Vicky, unable to tolerate her freedom of movement, unleashing the narrative drive that finally carries her to her death. On the other, there is the compulsion to repeat that animates the ballet company and Vicky as dancer. These divergences affect the closing sequences of the film.

Vicky's suicide closes the story's narrative line, bringing together, in Peter Brooks's terms, the story's end with a human end. But *The Red Shoes* complicates and elaborates this structural device. Vicky's death does not completely 'end' the film. The ballet of 'The Red Shoes', in which she had been about to dance, is not cancelled but is staged without its leading ballerina: a spotlight inscribes her absence into the performance. Here the ballet comes to represent the perpetual movement of narrative flow. But the ballet is itself actually about the drive towards death. It tells the story of the red dancing shoes that the heroine wants above all else and that then force her to dance until she dies. Vicky's last words, 'Take off the red shoes', acknowledge the metaphor. The red shoes, figured as desire and death simultaneously, allow the relationship between the two to be represented. The metonymic drive of desire, then transmuted into narrative movement, dances itself into its only possible stopping point: death itself. The ending of *The Red Shoes*, while acknowledging death as halt, also reaches out beyond its stillness into a celebration of the ballet as ceaseless change and repetition. The film combines the two opposing kinds of narrative evoked by Rivette, and the empty space under the spotlight cannot but conjure up the image of a girl dancing till the end of time.

In 'Beyond the Pleasure Principle', Freud gives a considerable amount of attention to the difficulty of relating the death drive to the pleasure principle, particularly the sexual instincts. The final opposition is not, as previously, between ego-instincts and sexual instincts but between life and death instincts. This tension recurs with the problem of narrative endings. For instance, Hollywood has been derided throughout its history for following the convention of the 'happy end', marked, at least in cliché, by the final kiss which fades out to 'The End'. But in some movies, a deviant doomed couple enables the two kinds of ending to fuse and the sexual drive of desire and the death drive are woven together in the 'dying together' ending. King Vidor's melodramatic Western *Duel in the Sun* (1947) ends like this: the doomed lovers Lewt and Pearl (Gregory Peck and Jennifer Jones) shoot at each other in a desolate mountain landscape. Wounded and bleeding, Pearl crawls towards her lover and they kiss passionately before dying in each other's arms. The narrative thus ends with a double 'human end' as well as the iconic Hollywood kiss, correctly and traditionally framed, which dissolves to the couple's death and, then, to the 'The End'.

In the B-movie sub-genre of doomed couples, the dying together motif is realized particularly appropriately through the motorcar that mobilizes and harnesses the death drive. The story's development extends into the movement of the car and the line of the road duplicates that of the narrative, both leading towards death and stasis. In this way, the car and the road link the narrative structure to thematic content, also generating an actual momentum and mobility from which these films derive their aesthetic specificity. The dying together ending accentuates the films' finality; neither hero nor heroine survives into a suggested 'after' to the story. The inevitability of death, furthermore, concentrates the plot in this single direction and contributes to the stylistic cohesion of the genre. For the Hollywood B movie there was neither time nor money for the more complex chain of events, the shifts in atmosphere or setting, the development of character, in more sophisticated movies. Fritz Lang's *You Only Live Once* (1937) is the prototype of the genre, followed by *They Live by Night* (Nicholas Ray, 1949) and *Gun Crazy* (Joseph H. Lewis, 1950). These dying together movies merge the death drive with the mobility of the plot, the motor car and the cinema. It was the concentrated, undiffused emotion of these movies and their minimalist attributes of style and of the story that ensured their influence on later art cinema.

This legacy is visible in Jean-Luc Godard's *Pierrot le Fou* (1965), which follows the literal, topographical, death drive of Hollywood's doomed couple movie. Godard takes the gangster road movie into the European art movie, once again with a car as figure for the motor force of desire. Ferdinand (Jean-Paul Belmondo) and Marianne (Anna Karina) reach the end of the road when they reach the Riviera, re-staging Charlton Heston and Jennifer Jones's ecstatic swerve into the sea in *Ruby Gentry* (King Vidor, 1952). From there, with a slow build-up of violence, the sea gradually comes to signify the point of narrative halt. *Pierrot le Fou* varies the convention of 'dying together'. In the first instance, the ending is closer to *Duel in the Sun*. Ferdinand shoots Marianne and then carries her to her deathbed, where she dies in his arms. But after Ferdinand's suicide, Godard ends the film with an image that turns away from the story and returns to cinema. The camera follows the smoke drifting away from the explosion with which Ferdinand kills himself, into the sky, which then turns into an empty frame of pure blue. Out of the emptiness, the lovers' voices whisper 'eternity', an image of formal stasis that transcends the metaphoric significance of death as narrative closure. The blank screen, simultaneously something and nothing, creates an ending that is purely cinematic, one that can only be given by cinema. The abstraction of pure light merges with the whiteness of the screen, as, for instance, in the endings of Jean-Marie Straub and Danielle Huillet's *The Bridegroom, Comedienne and the Pimp* and Hollis Frampton's *Zorn's Lemma*. The empty screen duplicates the still frame illuminated by the projector's beam, creating a return to the stasis of 'the end' that is derived from the cinema itself.

The death-drive tropes, the long car journey with a 'dying together' love story mapping the story's movement towards the sea, all represent ways in which cinema realizes the topographies of narrative structure. Takeshi Kitano's *Hana-Bi* (2000) creates a variation on these themes.[9] Whereas Brooks sees desire and Eros as the initial motor force of story-telling, only mutating into the death drive to signal 'ending', *Hana-Bi* has desire inextricably entwined with death as its opening premise. It is his love for his dying wife, Miyaki (Kayoko Kishimoto), that generates Nishi's (Kitano) impulse to movement, and he takes her on a last journey of happiness across Japan until they reach the sea. The journey is punctuated by violence, the residue of the gangster plot, but these eruptions of violence do not carry the inevitability of death that is represented by the wife's illness. The ending is marked geographically by a dead end, the sea, romantically by the couple's dying together, and in narrative by the chance presence of a little girl whose dance might suggest that 'life goes on'. The death, which is also metaphorically a ritual of remarriage, is the ending of Hawks or Hitchcock but makes a gesture to Renoir and Rossellini. From the start, the story is reconciled with its ending, which has already been accepted. In this sense, *Hana-Bi* realizes the Freudian 'death drive' narrative very closely.

For cinema, the movement and momentum that carry narrative desire into the space of the story's journey and the elongation of its delay echo its own movement. The representation of the end as death and quiescence can suggest a return of the repressed stillness on which cinema's illusion of movement depends. But the condensation of stillness, death and ending also works to mask the cinema's secret. Peter Brooks comments that when the drive of the narrative ends literally with death, the metonymic structure of narrative, its causal links, changes to the register of metaphor. Death marks the end but also the point 'beyond narratability'. The silence of 'The End' duplicates the silence of death itself but it also signifies total erasure, the nothing that lies beyond it. The story's chain of events, with their relation to metonymy and to the linkage of meaning and action, comes to a halt with an image in which a 'human end' stands in for the formal, structural, closure of the narrative. Just as the cinema offers a literal representation of narrative's movement out of an initial inertia, with its return to stasis narrative offers the cinema a means through which its secret stillness can emerge in a medium-specific form.

Garrett Stewart has argued that the cinema introduces another dimension to the metaphoric condensation between death and ending. The cinema's specificity is able to supply the perfect image for the metaphor: doubling up the 'end as death' with an image of death itself stilled by a freeze frame. As he discusses this death in freeze-frame ending, he too sees metaphor coming to replace metonymy:

> In the moment of mortal wounding, the contingencies of their narratives are over with those of their lives. Stop-action does just what its name suggests; it stops the narrative action not just the representation of activity. Hence the totalizing force of the freeze frame in such closing death scenes, its power to subsume narrative entirely to graphic figuration. Into the (metonomyic) chain of contiguity, continuous motion, of sequence, of plot, breaks the radical equation *stasis equals death*, the axis of substitution, the advent of metaphor.[10]

He points out that the force of the metaphor, the extra meaning given to the frozen cinematic image at this particular narrative point, masks the stillness of the filmstrip itself. The image takes on an almost literary inflexion that overwhelms its potential for self-reference. In the final freeze frame, in which the stillness of human death and the stasis of narrative closure coalesce in the (apparent) halting of cinematic flow, film can, in Garrett Stewart's words, 'subsume narrative into graphic figuration'. On the other hand, the affinity between cinema and story-telling, generally associated with movement, finds another aesthetic materialization at moments like these. The cinema's ability to create the frozen image of death brings with it the stillness of the photograph, which the powerful impact of 'ending' cannot completely subsume. As Stewart puts it:

> Between a film narrative's sustained enunciation and a film text's momentarily displayed constitution by photograms, between ocular effect and material basis, there opens the space for a theoretical interception of the text. It is at this level that the photogrammatic moment, even against the grain of narrative recuperation, may sometimes dynamite and anatomize a film's illusion of movement. For doesn't the held image occasionally remind us that the stillness

of photography, its halt and its hush, is never entirely shaken loose by sequential movement in and as film but is merely lost to view?[11]

While the 'held image' may well recall the 'stillness of photography' that insists beyond its narrative recuperation, the aesthetic of the photograph confuses the material nature of film. The freeze-frame ending leads in two directions, one that relates primarily to narrative and the other that relates to the materiality of film. First of all, the freeze frame represents the fusion between the death drive in narrative and the abrupt shift from the cinema's illusion of animated movement to its inorganic, inanimate state. This is the site of metaphor. Secondly, the freeze frame is a series of identical frames repeated in order to create an illusion of stillness to replace the illusion of movement. Beyond its presence as 'photograph', a single image outside the continuum of film, there is the continuous flow of the filmstrip and its individual frames, closing the gap between the film in the projector and the image on the screen. While the freeze frame brings finality to narrative, the sequence of individual frames can, as suggested by the system of pattern and repetition in the flicker film, lead to infinity. One direction finds a form to express 'the end' through metaphor. The other direction represents the aspiration to stories without end, a ceaseless metonymy. One leads to the famous freeze frames of the death-drive ending: for instance, *Butch Cassidy and the Sundance Kid* (1969) and *Thelma and Louise* (1991). The other leads to an uncertain future, a slight hint of an escape, for instance, in the first freeze-fame ending, when the child in Truffaut's *Les Quatre Cents Coups* (1959) turns to the camera or with the wife's outstretched hand in Satyajit Ray's *Charulata* (1964) or the freeze frame that brings a sudden halt to El Haji's humiliation in Ousmane Sembène's *Xala* (1975).

Two visual motifs in Michael Snow's *Wavelength* (1967) pay tribute to these two strands of cinema. The film weaves together reflections on both the infinite and the finite around the paradox of movement and stillness in the cinema. There is the forward drive of the zoom's movement, echoing the movement of narrative, promising a final destination and ending. There are frame flashes and sequences of frames coloured by filters indicating the presence of the filmstrip and the possibility of infinite series. The film begins with the zoom at its maximum width; a cupboard is carried into the loft that echoes with synchronized sound. Then the first sequence of flash frames and the start of the sine-wave soundtrack mark the transition into a different space and time in which cinema as camera movement and cinema as serial repetition work with and against each other. Forty-five minutes later, the zoom reaches its mechanical end and finds its visualized end.

Just as the mechanical movement of the zoom is comparable to the inexorable movement of the motor car in the death-drive movie, the movement forward in *Wavelength* across the loft also leads to a final stillness. This stillness is prefigured by a death. Approximately half way through the zoom's trajectory, a man stumbles into what is left of the loft space and falls to the floor. The 'death' functions as narrative punctuation and a thematic foreboding. It also introduces another temporal dimension: the presence of the past. As the camera continues its forward movement, the body disappears from view but remains as a memory of the space and time covered. The next character, and last to enter the frame, sees the corpse, now vanished from the path of the camera, as though she were looking back into the past events of a story. Her entry and exit are then 'ghosted' as her movement across the screen returns in superimposition. The shift from the straightforward register of the zoom to superimposition has a fundamental effect on the film's structure. The zoom has a shape and a destiny; it must reach a point of furthest extension and necessarily come to a full stop. However, the superimposition and its return not only suggest an infinitely repeatable past, but also the repetition inherent in the shape and pattern of a series. In the register of series, an image can be repeated infinitely, broken off by the arbitrary choice of the film-maker rather than by the completion of a pattern built into a mechanism or system. The suggestion of series, or sequence, then recalls the structure of the filmstrip, already depicted by flash frames.

The exact destination of the camera's movement is uncertain

until *Wavelength*'s closing minutes. When it does end, the image concentrates the contradictions in the cinema's relation to time. A still photograph of waves, the insubstantial combination of wind and water into perpetual motion, stops the movement of the zoom, the drive that had carried the camera forward from its point of departure, in its tracks. This image gives a twist to Deleuze's comments on the relation between the machine (motor car, train), water and cinema in his discussion of early French cinema:

> This was in no sense a renunciation of the mechanical: on the contrary, it was the transition from a mechanics of solids to a mechanics of fluids which, from a concrete point of view, was to find a new extension of the quantity of the movement as a whole. It provided better conditions to pass from the concrete to the abstract, a greater possibility of communicating an irreversible duration to movements, independently of their figurative characters, a more certain power of extracting movement from the thing that moved.[12]

Michael Snow's ending assumes the mechanics of fluids and turns them back to solids. *Wavelength* ends by going beyond the camera's literal movement, the concrete, towards a level of abstraction that is, itself, searching for a beyond to 'irreversible duration'. The film, in a sense, is a reflection on the cinema's ability to bring light and movement and the machine into a dialectical relationship.

As the zoom closes in on its appropriate final image, the superimposition effect once again subordinates finality to repetition until both camera movement and superimposition turn into a freeze frame. This is the freeze-frame ending that Garrett Stewart sees as stillness and death. A photograph that shows perpetual motion, and ironically suggests the 'liquid' motion of cinema, is transformed into the sequence of identical images that constitute the freeze frame, and thus returns to cinema as filmstrip rather than camera movement. Unlike the photograph, cinema cannot but come to an end. In its final moments, *Wavelength* brings movement and stillness into a dynamic relation with each other and with the representation of time. The 45-minute (spatially continuous, temporally discontinuous) zoom has a beginning, a middle and an end that structure the shape of the film as a whole. But the series of repeated, superimposed images check the unstoppable movement of the zoom, exposing it to an encounter with series and infinity. As the sine-wave dies out on the sound-track, the sound of police sirens comes in, bringing back in memory the human story and the human death, its trace once again duplicating the stasis of narrative closure. The death-drive narrative structure finds its ending in stillness, haunted by the memory of a human end. Here is finality. On the other hand, there is sequence, repetition and the photograph of waves. This meeting of movement stilled and the still in movement coexist simultaneously within different time structures. In a dynamic or dialectical relationship, time is neither tied to the index and the past nor entirely freed from it; time is subordinated to the linearity of narrative movement and moves beyond and outside it.

Chapter Five

Alfred Hitchcock's *Psycho* (1960)

Thinking about *Psycho* across a gap of more than 44 years, after the centenary of cinema and into the new millennium, its significance as a milestone waxes rather than wanes. *Psycho* represents a moment of change in the history of the film industry. It stands on the edge of the divide: metonymically, it reaches back to the chronicle of cinema with which Hitchcock himself is so inextricably imbricated, but it also stands, metaphorically, for a decisive break with that kind of cinema. The crisis in the old Hollywood film industry, caught at a crossroads, faced with its own mortality, gave him the opportunity to write its epitaph, but also to transcend its conventions and create something startling and new. With a return to the studio and to black-and-white film stock, *Psycho* harks back to an earlier era for Hollywood, but its low-budget, scaled-down production values chimed with the emergence of new forces: television, of course, but also low-budget American independents and European art cinema. The film produces a sense of the 'new' out of a rearrangement of the 'old', reusing narrative and other motifs that are familiar from across the body of Hitchcock's work.

In the first instance, *Psycho* is a highly formal, minimalist film. Located firmly within traditional narrative, it nevertheless attains a modern self-reflexivity. Pared down to the limit, the story's pattern draws attention to itself, revealing a skeletal shape usually concealed by the clutter of surrounding narrative detail. There is nothing new in the generic plots Hitchcock draws on in *Psycho*. He had always used traditional forms of story-telling and translated these non-cinematic forms onto the space of the cinema screen in ways that meshed with cinema's proclivity for movement, mystery and shock. Furthermore, in the relative freedom of his production conditions, he was able to exploit the narrow border where accumulated cultural connotation overlaps with more sophisticated psychoanalytic material. *Psycho* was Hitchcock's opportunity to bring his longstanding themes and motifs to the surface. These two sides, the form of the film and its psychoanalytic content, are inextricably connected. In a literal sense *Psycho* is a death-drive movie and the associated motifs not only appear in Marion's story but also in the final revelation of the ending. However, when Marion's murder halts the film's narrative, changing its structure, the topography also shifts and the death-drive story opens into a space of the uncanny.

In both sections of the film, the story is articulated into a visual lexicon. The road, the traversing of exterior space, is designed to convey a journey; the house conveys mystery and an interior space. Both are visualized through the use of back projection and studio sets from which unnecessary exterior intrusion is eliminated. This fusion of image and idea illustrates Gilles Deleuze's vision of Hitchcock as standing on the frontier between action and mental image, pushing the movement image to its limit: 'It was Hitchcock's task to introduce the mental image to the cinema' and 'In Hitchcock . . . all is interpretation, from beginning to end.'[1] Hitchcock, the consummate story-teller, turns back on himself, as it were, in a meditation on the mechanics of story-telling that he knew so well. As Deleuze points out, this development assumes an audience that is able to follow his moves. Not only does he introduce his public to the process of interpretation in his films, but he also appeals to their own deep cultural experience of story-telling and its conventions, that is, to his and their shared traditions. *Psycho* makes use of the most recognizable of narrative figures and tropes, of near-cliché images associated with the topographies of narrative movement and investigation.

Marion's death signals a pivotal point in *Psycho* that brings formal questions about the structure of narrative into the very surface

The space of movement in
Psycho.

of its plot. But it also mobilizes the imagery of movement and stillness that had taken Marion from Phoenix onto the road into the
imagery of the transition from life to death that is so central to the
film. The homology that connects 'stillness', 'death' and 'ending'
takes the fiction film, which generally conceals its material base,
back to the secret stillness that lies concealed within it. At the very
heart of *Psycho* is the shock of Marion's murder. In the aftermath of
this explosion of violence, there is a momentary pause to register
her transition from living human being, in whose story the audience has been deeply involved, to corpse. Hitchcock was deeply
preoccupied by this moment, in which he broke with tradition to
kill off the character played by his star.

Hitchcock extended the transition from life to death into the
surrounding *mise en scène*. For a moment, the stillness of the
recently animate body is juxtaposed with the stream of water still
pouring from the shower, inanimate material in unrelenting movement. First, in close-up, the water runs down the drain, creating a
circular axis that the camera echoes just before this image
dissolves. The circular movement prefigures the next close-up on
Marion's eye. As the involuntary flickering of the eye is usually a
guarantee of life itself, its fixed, inanimate stare becomes uncanny.
Just when the image's stillness seems necessarily to derive from a
photograph, a single drop of water falls in front of the camera. Its
effect is to reanimate the image, to create another contrast with the
inanimate corpse. The paradox of the cinema's uncertain boundary

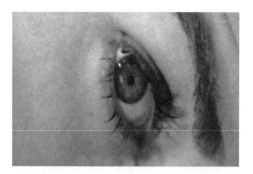

The stillness of death.

between stillness and movement also finds a fleeting visibility. The stillness of the 'corpse' is a reminder that the cinema's living and moving bodies are simply animated stills and the homology between stillness and death returns to haunt the moving image. Janet Leigh, in her account of making *Psycho*, emphasizes the enormous importance of this scene. She describes her discussions with Hitchcock in which they foresaw the scene's difficulty. She says that initially he had hoped to have special contact lenses made that would hold her eyes open in the stillness of death. But, since the process would have taken too long for their schedule, it was ultimately 'up to her'. It was, indeed, one of the most troublesome shots in the film. Janet Leigh describes not being able to breathe or swallow or blink as the cameraman worked in close-up, pulling focus while also moving the camera. It took somewhere between 22 and 26 takes and she attributes the successful one to a combination of luck and desperation.[2] Looking closely at the film, her stillness is so deathly that it almost seems as though Hitchcock had substituted a still photograph for the living actress.

Immediately after the murder, a 'pivot' shot organizes the transition from one plot segment to the next. At the same time, the image of death is woven from the shot of Marion's body into the story's wider themes and structure. The camera's actual movement creates the pivot, turning around in the space of the room to trace the narrative's move from its first into its second phase, from murder to mystery. The close-up of Marion's face as she lies dead

The space of the uncanny.

on the bathroom floor is the point of departure for the transitional shot which then passes over the sign of Marion's aspiration (the stolen money), and moves up to the window in order to frame the image of the Bates house. This sequence shot (three pieces of film amalgamated into the appearance of a single movement) translates its three emblematic images from literal object into narrative idea, as the initial impetus of the story mutates into something else. The film's psychoanalytic material that will revolve around the uncanny is signalled by the image of the house shot from the window of Marion's hotel room. Marion's story and her body are thus displaced, in visual image and narrative, onto the enigma 'Mother'. This next phase of *Psycho*'s story will also lead inexorably towards a figure of death that Marion's murder has prefigured. But this next movement is not so much towards death but towards the dead, the uncannily preserved human body that bears witness to the human mind's resistance to death. This is, of course, the mother's body and the ultimate problem of death, the end, becomes conflated with that other problem, the maternal and human beginnings.

The pivot shot that organizes the transition between the film's two sections also divides the two kinds of plot that Hitchcock has pared down and streamlined into skeletal form. Peter Wollen argued, in a short but suggestive article in 1981, that *Psycho* is a narrative hybrid, combining two plot types: the fairy-tale and the detective story. The two types differ in their relation to time and space. The fairy-tale is linear and horizontal. A journey into a no man's land, suggesting that 'civilisation anywhere is a thin crust', leads to adventure, to confrontation with and defeat of a villain, to the rescue of the heroine and marriage. Wollen uses Vladimir Propp's morphology of narrative to characterize this fairy-tale plot. The morphology also has a built-in topography: the hero moves away from his original home (in the beginning) to found a new one (the end). The road along which he travels from one point to the other marks both his journey and the linear movement of the plot itself. Wollen relates the detective story, on the other hand, to time:

> As Michel Butor was the first to point out, there is always a double story, the story of an investigation ends with the telling of another story embedded in it, the story of a crime. The narrative of one story concludes with the narration of another.[3]

This story of investigation looks backwards, searching for and deciphering clues in order to reconstruct events that have already taken place. While the movement of the journey story is across space and looks forward, that of the detective story looks backward and into time. The detective story necessarily brings with it a certain abstraction. Since its aim is to expose a hidden secret, its backward look involves repetition, a literal retracing of the victim and villain's steps and movements. Wollen argues that the fairy-tale plot characterizes Marion's journey and the detective plot characterizes her sister Lila's investigation.

Peter Brooks draws attention to the suggestive nature of the word 'plot' in English.[4] Its first two meanings refer to space: a plot of land and a ground plan or diagram. Its second two are more abstract: the series of events outlining a narrative and a secret plan to accomplish a hostile or illegal purpose. In Hitchcock's hybrid plots, the space of terrain crossed by a journey, is literally 'plotted' by the hero's movement, while the space of the secret plan belongs to the mind of the plotter and the deciphering powers of the detective. In between the two, slips become clues. One is associated with the movement forward of action, the other is associated with the movement backward of detection. One is associated with the principle of movement-gendered male in traditional narrative structure, while the other is non-gender specific and associated with curiosity and deciphering.

Psycho takes the plots that characterized Hitchcock's British thriller series, which he continued to recycle in Hollywood, and uses them in a way that is shocking both in its novelty and in its strange familiarity.[5] There are similar plots in, for instance, *The 39 Steps* (1935) and *North by Northwest* (1959). But in *Psycho* there is a crucial formal twist. Rather than carefully integrated and inter-woven, the two patterns are separated neatly, splitting the story across each side of the murder. Marion's journey dominates the first third while the rest is dominated by Lila's investigation into her death. This division is the cornerstone that allows two plot structures to emerge, no longer just a hidden skeleton, into a visible form. Marion's section of the story establishes its point of departure, Phoenix, her home where she lives with her sister and mother. Her story has, as its unfulfilled destination, her fiancé and the new home she hopes to make with him out of the stolen money. Her story is traced, or plotted, along the roads from Arizona to California along which she travels. Lila's investigative section of the story circles around the Bates house and motel that conceals, not only the mystery of Marion's death, but also the further mystery of Mrs Bates, seen to be alive but known to be dead. The stretch of the road that leads to Marion's death is echoed by the stretch back in time to an 'Ur-death', a long-guarded secret: the crime of matricide. These topographies, of course, are far from specific to cinema or to Hitchcock. But in translating the themes, forms and metaphors of popular story-telling, he rendered them visually and physically into a *mise en scène*, for the spectator's eye and then for the mind's eye. *Psycho*'s sparseness and the separation of the two plot patterns enhance their visibility. It is as though Hitchcock, in addition to transposing his shots from a graphic, story-boarded form to celluloid, also visualized the patterns of his plots in terms of these kinds of figuration.

As Jacques Rivette points out, Hitchcock's stories end with 'a marriage, a death or a revelation'.[6] These structural forms are consciously inserted into *Psycho*. Hitchcock makes crystal clear the 'pathetic' relation between marriage and death as endings. Marion's journey from Phoenix, should, according to the conventional pattern, end with marriage, with a new home symmetrical to the one left behind. Marriage has, from the very opening scene with Sam, been established as Marion's explicit desire. She no longer simply wants his love and to continue their affair; she wants to get married and the money that Marion steals was to be a wedding present. And marriage is the 'happy ending' that Hitchcock used in most of his movies, not simply as a gesture to the conventions of production codes but as a profound gesture to the narrative desire to 'end', the entropy that pursues its dynamic movement.

In *Psycho*, the fairy-tale model assumes structural attributes associated with the death-drive model. The *Psycho* plot is activated by Marion's desire, which translates into a metonymic figure in the journey, her drive from Arizona to California. But the drive and the motor car as literal and narrative engine lead to stillness. The car's halt joins Marion in death as they, life and machine, share a common grave in the swamp. Although Hitchcock's 'killing off' of Marion does, indeed, contravene the conventions of Hollywood and the traditions of story-telling, the conflation between marriage and death makes a radical, but formal, point about narrative structure. Desire for marriage, and for the happy ending, are not simply dispersed through a naturalistic device but violently truncated and superimposed. The interchangeability of death and marriage, functioning as figures of ending, is dramatized, ironically and tragically. Here *Psycho* deviates from the pattern discussed by Brooks. The plot is momentarily lost as its metonymy collapses without the satisfaction of death displaced into the metaphor of ending. In *Psycho*, Marion has tried to appropriate the principle of action and movement, and uneasiness is mixed with a slight element of thrill as her voice-over imagines the impact of her sudden departure and the reactions of the men she encountered on the way. From this perspective, Marion's action must be understood as a transgression in terms of both the law and the gender principles of traditional narrative structure. Her tragedy is that she encounters her aberrant complement: the man who has been unable to establish himself as the subject of movement and is trapped in the space of the maternal home. When she turns off into the side road leading to the Bates Motel, long bypassed by a new main road, she moves into the uncertain space of the uncanny.

With *Psycho*, Hitchcock not only brought death to the foreground of the plot but also the question of its cinematic staging. Here he was able to strip away the armature of romance with which Hollywood, and popular story-telling in general, sugared the sight and site of violent death. In the fairy-tale, the villain's death was an essential component in narrative closure, to be followed by the hero and heroine united and living happily ever after. In most Hitchcock thrillers, the villain's pursuit and death has a similar structural function. But as he invests such spectacle, suspense and drama in the death of the villain, these scenes very often constitute the visual climax to the film as a whole. Their complex staging often takes place in public so that the spectacle has its own built-in or ready-made audience: for instance, the dance hall in *Young and Innocent* (1936), the fairground in *Strangers on a Train* (1951), the Albert Hall in both versions of *The Man Who Knew Too Much* (1934/1956), the presidents' heads in *North by Northwest* (1959). *Blackmail* (1929), *Murder* (1930), *Saboteur* (1942) and *To Catch a Thief* (1955) all end with, or threaten, death by falling as a public spectacle. As the spectacle of death constitutes the high point of many Hitchcock plots, the end of the villain's life comes to duplicate 'The End' of the story itself. In a sense, these extraordinary tableaux animated by suspense and anxiety overwhelm the actual closing moments of a movie. The ultimate figuration of narrative closure, the 'formation of the couple' (or in Vladimir Propp's terms 'function Wedding'), takes up comparatively little and unspectacular screen time. It was, perhaps, natural for Hitchcock to associate the villain's death with spectacle; public execution in London had ceased only about 50 years before he was born.

Hitchcock always seemed to feel that the audience for the spectacular aspects of his films would be wandering somewhere between peep-show, roller-coaster and gallows. While the closing death of the villain lies directly in this lineage, there is a significant stylistic shift in the staging of death in *Psycho*.

Marion's murder, located in the modern context of the motel, is linked to the Victorian atmosphere of the Bates house by the predatory stuffed birds, prefiguring the murder and figuring the illusion of life after death that Mrs Bates will come to personify. As a murder, it must, of course, be secret and has a different narrative function from the death of the villain. But cinematically her death is given a spectacular staging. The complex, almost baroque, surroundings and the theatricality that have contributed to the spectacle of death in so many earlier Hitchcock movies have disappeared, leaving only the formal whiteness of the shower, the woman's naked body, the flow of blood and water and the screech of the violins. The sense of death as public spectacle has been replaced by a more abstract, cinematic, spectacle. It is the cinema spectator alone who can interpret this complex montage sequence. Although the montage sequence in *Psycho* had many successors, it is hard to think of precedents in the cinema that followed the conversion to sound. It is tempting to imagine that, when Hitchcock asked Saul Bass to design the sequence, he had in mind films that he had watched at the London Film Society during the late 1920s. There he had seen how Eisenstein translated the eruption of violence into fragments of film and turned shock into the cinema of attractions.

Marion's death marks 'the end' for the journey that had driven her story, but produces the narrative's new phase in which the drive of desire is replaced by the drive of curiosity and detection. Her disappearance is the initial enigma that then fuels the investigative phase of the story. Taking place, as it does, in the centre of the movie, the double function of Marion's death confirms, from a formal perspective, the 'hybridity' of *Psycho*. When Lila replaces Marion as the film's protagonist, her desire to discover her sister's fate continues its drive but profoundly affects the aesthetics of the narrative. A circling movement concentrated increasingly on the Bates house and motel replaces the horizontal direction of the road and its forward movement. The story's shift in spatial direction brings with it a temporal shift. From a story looking towards the future and its protagonist's happy end it turns into a story looking back, attempting to decipher the events of the past. Lila's investigation into the recent past unwittingly exposes another, archaic, past hidden in the Bates house, going beyond the secret space of the detective story into the space of the unconscious. This layer of the story, a psychotic relation between mother and son, opens into the archaic uncanny that Freud would have recognized. In Hitchcock's telling of this story, the language of the cinema plays both a mediating and a metaphoric role. Although two patterns divide the larger framework of the film's narrative, they are themselves framed by two opening and closing camera movements, in which the camera itself takes over as the film's narrator.[7] These camera movements embed the story firmly within the cinema's own capacity to create meaning and further enact the figure of a 'drive'.

Psycho opens with a series of camera movements that select an upper window in a Phoenix hotel and move through the window to penetrate the space and privacy of the couple inside. This act of penetration prefigures subsequent violations of space throughout the rest of the movie, of which the violent intrusion into the enclosed space of the shower, combined with the knife's penetration of Marion's body, are the most remarkable and shocking. But although the camera subsequently latches onto smaller, or minor, movements of story, character or point of view, this opening sequence sets in motion the transcendent drive towards an end that is finally realized in the film's closing sequence. In its last shot, a long, slow tracking movement, the film reaches the image that will allow it to come to a halt: the close-up of Norman/Mother looking straight into camera. Just as the audience's look had been drawn into that first movement, detached from any character point of view, so it is inscribed into its last. Movement reaches towards stillness and then towards the dead: Mother's skull appears superimposed briefly on Norman's features and they merge. But the film marks 'THE END' with its ultimate shot, which encapsulates movement stilled, the animate transformed into the inanimate, the organic into the inorganic. These opening and closing camera movements meet in the pivotal sequence that follows the murder, when the camera transfers the story line from Marion's journey to the Bates house. And the final shot of Marion's car returns to and reiterates death as the drive of narrative.

Peter Wollen concludes his article on 'Hybrid Plots in Psycho' as follows:

> *Psycho*, I think, is the most extreme case of a film . . . in which the fairy-tale is not simply a hybrid with the tale of detection, but is also transformed into a different type of story which, following Freud, we can call a tale of the uncanny.[8]

The uncanny has long contributed to popular culture. A 'popular culture of the uncanny' prefigured the genre of 'horror' with which Hitchcock was experimenting in *Psycho*. For the 'Gothic' of the late eighteenth century, abandoned sites of human habitation provided a style, vocabulary and topography for this sense of nameless dread. During the period when he was developing the *Psycho* project, Hitchcock had been impressed by the success of the French import *Les Diaboliques* (Henri Clouzot, 1954) and by Roger Corman's adaptation of the stories of Edgar Allan Poe into low-budget movies for American International Pictures. The new horror genre bore witness to the continued public interest in the uncanny and its licence to explore areas of dread and superstition banished by the rational and the everyday. *Psycho*'s uncanny turns towards the archaic and the Gothic.

Freud's discussion of the uncanny initially focuses on two meanings of the German word *heimlich*. The first has various associations with the homely, the familiar; the second has associations with the secret, something that must be concealed and kept out of public sight. The two, while apparently unconnected in meaning, are connected by topography: the home *encloses* and thus gives comfort while the secret is *enclosed* and thus hidden.[9] These two meanings are fused in the closing moments of *Psycho*'s pivotal shot, bringing into a single image the dual significance that the Bates house will have for the rest of the film. It is Norman's home, his mother's home, yet it is also the place where the story's ultimate enigma lies hidden. But the secret concealed in the Bates house conforms to two further aspects of the uncanny. Freud identifies the body of the mother as the first 'home', and thus familiar, but with the passing of time this *heimlichkeit* has become archaic, *unheimlich*. Secondly, Freud comments on the uncanniness of the corpse, the inanimate residue of a once living being. Norman's mother, of course, is a 'mummified' corpse. In the last resort, the film's uncanny is associated with the maternal. There seems to be almost a touch of parody in Hitchcock's manipulation of these themes, especially with the Bates house's Gothic connotations, evoking the 'haunted house' in its design and *mise en scène*. Even the motel, 'left behind' when the highway moved, has this sense of the once-familiar that has been extracted, like a ruin, from the flow of life; Norman's everyday performance of his pointless chores seems to take on an aura of repetition compulsion. Freud's interest in the topic revolves around a return of the repressed, of something ancient, that had once been known and reassuring but had become a source of dread. In *Psycho*, the aesthetics of the uncanny have their roots in that emblem of the ancient and the repressed: the maternal body and its decay.[10]

The association between the maternal body and the uncanny had appeared before in Hitchcock films and has a relation to his depiction of women more generally. In *Psycho*, 'mother' as site of horror and madness brings back memories of Uncle Charlie's phobia in *Shadow of a Doubt* (1943), made at the height of American anxiety about 'Momism'. In *Notorious* (1946), Mrs Sebastian, who prefigures aspects of the psychic structures of *Psycho*, adds foreignness to the maternal uncanny. The glamorous beauty of Hitchcock's blonde stars had acted as a veil for that other, repressed, side of the female body: the uncanny body of the mother. In his 1950s films, and with Grace Kelly in particular, Hitchcock streamlined the star iconography of the 'cool blonde'. High production values went hand in hand with the highly censored but all-pervading eroticism that was symptomatic of America as it celebrated its status as the 'democracy of glamour' in its Cold War with Communism. This is the cinema, with its witty, self-conscious voyeurism, on which Hitchcock turned his back with *Psycho*. Both Janet Leigh as Marion and Vera Miles as Lila are taken out of the high production values associated with Hitchcock's usual blondes. Janet Leigh describes the meticulous research that went into the lower-middle-class 'ordinariness' of Marion's character so that her blondeness became a simple characteristic rather than an iconographic emblem.

It is as though the disappearance of the fetishized female star had enabled investigation of the maternal uncanny and its relation to the space of the home. While a topographical similarity connects the space of the home to the space of secrets, secrets are the product of the home, the domestic, the family. As Norman explains: '*This place* is my home . . . *this place* happens to be my only world. I grew up in that house up there. I had a very happy childhood. My mother and I were more than happy.' Behind Norman's words lie the trauma and repression that, in Freud's terms, turn the *heimlich* space (homely / concealed) into the *unheimlich* space of the uncanny. The bond between mother and son, on the one hand the most normal of relations, is, on the other, easily distorted into the perverse, so that the home conceals deviance and then the enigma: the crime of matricide. The detective Arbogast's and then Lila's investigation of the Bates house, the enclosed space of the uncanny, is also an incursion into the privacy of Norman's world. The point of view tracking shot with which Hitchcock stages Lila's journey up the hill, cuts between her, looking up towards the house, and the house itself, which seems to draw her, just as her curiosity drives her, towards its secret.

When Lila enters Mrs Bates's bedroom, her pressing concern for her sister is temporarily suspended. At the same time, the inexorable movement of the plot, carrying her towards direct, face-to-face encounter with Mrs Bates also falters. Lila's curiosity roams freely around the house. On a literal level, these scenes build suspense through delay, but they also elongate her journey through the uncanny. Although her point of view organizes the sequence, it is no longer attached to the tracking shot that has taken her to the door. Her look becomes a surrogate for the spectator's desire to see inside this forbidden and frightening space. Mrs Bates's bedroom is, of course, maintained as if she were alive: washbasin, fireplace and clothes all ready for use. But the only sign of human presence is the strange fossil-like impression of a body left on the bed. Hitchcock isolates two details: first a fast tracking shot moves into a close-up of a perfectly lifelike metal reproduction of hands folded on a cushion; secondly, Lila is suddenly startled by her reflection in a mirror. Freud mentions both, the lifelike metal reproduction of limbs and the sudden sight of one's own reflection, in his consideration of various uncanny phenomena. Norman's bedroom, with its objects suspended somewhere between childhood and adolescence, is subjected to Lila's curiosity. Inexorably, Lila's detour comes to an end, and the movement of this segment of the film returns to its ultimate uncanny: Mother's preserved corpse in the cellar.

Until the very last moment, *Psycho* preserves an element of doubt that prepares the way for the film's actual secret: that Mrs Bates is both alive and dead. When Lila finds Mrs Bates in the cellar, the old woman seems to move, to respond to her voice and her touch. Then, as the corpse turns and the skull looks directly into the camera, the swinging light bulb seems to animate the inanimate body. This fleeting moment is, in a certain sense, a gesture of horror in which the blurred boundary between the stillness of the corpse and its fake movement is enacted with truly Gothic effect. Raymond Bellour reflects on the implications of this moment, pointing out that the light is concentrated on the wall in front of Mrs Bates, as though on a cinema screen, placing 'Mother' in the position of the spectator who is then faced with:

> his mirror image (the fetish inhabited by the death wish) when she looks at him directly during the next two close-up shots. This is particularly true the second time, when Lila's terror causes her to knock

against the light bulb, making it swing back and forth. The vacillation in the lighting thus produced is repeated and amplified . . . the skull seems to be animated by this vibration – this play of lights and shadows that also signifies the cinema itself.[11]

An image of stillness, and stillness duplicating the stasis of narrative closure, is finally enacted in Norman's mind through his own, internal, blurring of the inanimate with the animate. This final drama is introduced by the psychiatrist's summing up ('Norman had to keep alive the illusion of his mother being alive'). His speech leads to the image of Norman in his cell, and 'Mother's' decision to remain completely still. ('I'll just sit and stare like one of his stuffed birds.') In the last resort, the second segment of *Psycho* fuses two motifs. First of all, there is a gesture towards the death-drive ending, the image of the mortal body, which returns in the film's last image of Marion's car emerging from the swamp. This ending emerges out of the more disturbing conflation between Norman and Mother that blurs the boundary, not only between mother and son, but between the animate and the inanimate, the living and the dead. And this, after all, is the boundary that the cinema itself blurs:

Film is no longer content to preserve the object, enshrouded as it were in the instant, as the bodies of insects are preserved intact, out of the distant past, in amber . . . Now, for the first time the image of things is also the image of their durations, change mummified as it were.[12]

Bazin's observation seems strangely appropriate to *Psycho*. Norman's taxidermy preserves the bodies of birds out of the past and his preservation of Mother's body, of course, plays on the pun with 'mummified'. But Bazin's phrasing also points to the cinema's blurred boundary. His image of change is an image of death and evokes the way that, when Mother takes over and inhabits Norman, the dead merges with the living and movement merges with stillness.

In 1993 (at the Kunstmuseum, Wolfsburg) Douglas Gordon exhibited an installation piece, *24-Hour Psycho*, which expands Hitchcock's original by slowing it down electronically from its original 90 minutes to 24 hours. Naturally, these viewing conditions erode the tightly drawn, graphic structure of the original story line and its reference to traditional narrative genres. However, Hitchcock's filming practice has left its imprint in the formal, linear quality of the images, their stark contrasts of light and shade, reflecting the carefully designed images, always patiently story-boarded before filming and with a preference for back projection, especially in *Psycho*. This work creates a dialogue between the film and technology to discover something that is not there in the original as screened but can be revealed within it. The installation has a reverie-producing effect, especially in the light of changes that have taken place in film consumption since 1960. During the 20 years leading up to the cinema's centenary in 1995–6, video had transformed the ways in which film could be watched, introducing the spectator to a new kind of control over the image and its flow. *24-Hour Psycho* is, as much as anything, a celebration of the radical new possibilities offered by video viewing. Douglas Gordon had happened to reverse his *Psycho* tape to freeze-frame the scene in which Norman watches Marion through the peephole, and then, it is said, accidentally discovered the beauty of the film when run at two frames per second.

As Amy Taubin has pointed out, *24-Hour Psycho* opened up a Hollywood genre movie to the aesthetics of slow motion and thus to the traditions of the avant-garde film.[13] She comments on the way that the work, beyond its slow motion, seems to take the cinema, paradoxically refracted through an electronic medium, back to its own materiality and yield up the stillness of the individual frame in the filmstrip:

> By slowing the film down to a 13th of its normal speed, Gordon shows us not a 'motion picture' but a succession of stills, each projected for about half a second. We become aware of the intermittency of the film image and the fragility of the illusion of real time in motion pictures.[14]

Here the cinema can find a way back to its essential stillness and the double temporality to which Taubin refers. While the flow of the image at 24 frames a second tends to assert a 'now-ness' to the picture, stillness allows access to the time of the film's registration, its 'then-ness'. This is the point, essentially located in the single frame, where the cinema meets the still photograph, both registering a moment of time frozen and thus fossilized.

But, inexorably, a reverie triggered by *24-Hour Psycho* must be affected by the presence of death that pervades it, hovering somewhere between the stillness of the photograph and the movement of the cinema. In Douglas Gordon's reworking, in *Psycho* itself and in Hitchcock's films more generally, stories, images and themes of death accumulate on different levels, leading like threads back to the cinema, to reflect on its deathly connotations as a medium and ultimately its own mortality. Just as *Psycho*, in 1960, marked a final staging post in the history of the studio system as the basis for the Hollywood film industry, *24-Hour Psycho*, like an elegy, marks a point of no return for the cinema itself.

In an art gallery, the spectator watches Gordon's reflection on the slow-motion effect, unable (as in the cinema) to intervene in the projection flow. But *24-Hour Psycho* is also a significant, and a *public*, meditation on new forms of *private* spectatorship. Anyone who wants to is now able to play with the film image and, perhaps, in the process, evolve voyeurism and investment in spectacle into something closer to fetishism and investment in repetition, detail and personal obsession. Gordon's own discovery of another dimension to the film image, as he slowed his machine to examine a highly self-reflexive moment of voyeurism, can stand symbolically for this shift in spectatorship. *24-Hour Psycho* may represent an elegiac moment for the cinema, but it also marks a new dawn, the beginning of an 'expanded cinema', which will grow in possibility as electronic technologies are overtaken by digital ones. In this aesthetic juncture André Bazin's perception of the cinema takes on a new relevance as it is possible to watch the slow process of mutation as 'the image of things is also the image of their durations' and the process of 'change mummified' becomes a spectacle in its own right.

Chapter Six

Roberto Rossellini's *Journey to Italy / Viaggio in Italia* (1953)

While Hitchcock's innovation in *Psycho* is derived from a tightened, streamlined narrative, shot almost exclusively on set, some years earlier Rossellini had created a landmark film by, on the contrary, loosening the lines of narrative, displacing its drive, shooting casually in city streets. But both films have certain structures and thematic preoccupations in common. Both revolve around an initial journey that leads, after a halt, to a space of the uncanny. In *Psycho* this is a space of suspense dominated by the uncanny of the maternal body in which the archaic material revealed relates only to the unconscious. In *Journey to Italy* the space is dominated by the ruins and traces of an ancient civilization. Rossellini used this terrain to extend into cinema the blurred boundaries between the material and the spiritual, reality and magic, and between life and death that Bazin and Barthes associated with photography. In both films, however, death forms a central thematic element and both films enable the cinema's paradoxical relation between movement and stillness to achieve a degree of visibility.

In *Journey to Italy*, Rossellini used the environs of Naples, the sites and ruins of the area, to bring the presence of the city's past into the film, almost like an essay woven into the story. Ingrid Bergman remembered Rossellini's long-standing interest in this particular region:

> He adored Pompeii. He knew everything about it. He was only look-
> ing for a story into which he could put Pompeii and the museums

The excavation: Pompeii.

and Naples and all that Naples stands for which he was always fascinated with because the people of Naples are different from the people in Rome or Milano. He wanted to show all those grottoes with the relics and the bones and the museums and the laziness of all the statues.[1]

Rossellini was interested in the paradoxes associated with Vesuvius, the material traces of the past, the immaterial presence of the dead that haunt memory, religion and superstition. *Journey to Italy* was a source of bewilderment while in production, seemingly aimless and almost plotless, leaving its stars struggling for direction. On similar grounds it was dismissed on release, with only a few critics understanding that it was carefully constructed to undermine conventions of event-driven narrative and open out space and time for thought. The places included in the film were carefully chosen for their resonances and associations, from which Rossellini creates an implicit, idiosyncratic, commentary on the cinema, its reality, its indexical quality, as well as its uncanny ability to preserve life.

Some of these themes come together in the Pompeii sequence towards the end of *Journey to Italy*. The film's protagonists, the English couple Alex and Katherine Joyce (played by George Sanders and Ingrid Bergman), are taken to witness a dramatic excavation at Pompeii. Over time, the bodies buried by lava had disintegrated, leaving behind a void, as in the contours of a mould,[2] which was then carefully filled with liquid plaster. When hardened, the mould would be uncovered and the imprint of the figures revealed. It was the final stage of the process, the slow uncovering of the plaster cast, that Alex and Katherine have been invited to witness. Finally, the figures are uncovered and, in the words of one of the workmen, they see 'A couple, a man and a woman, perhaps husband and wife, just as they were at the moment of death'. Due to the suddenness of the eruption, the figures uncovered at Pompeii are preserved as they died, caught in the moment of transition between life and death. Here, the figures are lying side by side, stretching towards each other as though the impact of the lava had snatched one from the other's embrace. Raymond Bellour comments on the scene: 'There emerges the form of a couple clasped in an embrace, as a picture appears in a developer. Thus, a photograph is formed from the real itself.'[3] The plaster casts, formed from the imprint left by an original object, are, like photographs, indexical images.

In 1952, when Rossellini was shooting *Journey to Italy*, the excavations in Pompeii had only just resumed after the war. He had good contacts with the archaeologists and made sure that he would be informed of significant discoveries in time to film them. Rossellini clearly felt that the tragedy of Pompeii was essential to his film. He stands within the tradition, perhaps its last representative, of the fascination that the buried town had exerted on European intellectuals. It is a fossil of the ancient civilizations that signified so much for different waves of Enlightenment culture.[4] But it also brings with it the shudder of the uncanny, the return of the repressed, the presence of the dead, the difficulty of understanding death and time itself. Anthony Vidler describes this history:

> This dramatic confrontation of the homely and the unhomely made Pompeii a locus for the literary and artistic uncanny for much of the nineteenth century . . . *L'étrange, l'inquiétant, das Unheimlich*, all found their natural place in stories that centered on the idea of history suspended, the dream come to life, the past restored to the

present . . . The special characteristic of this retrospective vision was its unsettling merging of past and present, its insistence on the rights of the unburied dead. In Pompeii, it seemed, history, that solid real of explanation and material fact, was taking a kind of revenge on its inventors.[5]

'The idea of history suspended, the dream come to life, the past restored to the present', these images of the excavated town might also be used to describe the cinema's unique ability to confuse time. As people and history recede into the past, the traces they leave on the world mark their absence, the impossibility of regaining time, but also bear witness to the reality of their once-upon-a-time presence. With the cinema, the past is preserved in the full appearance of reality. In the Pompeii sequence, filmed in 1952, with the living presence of the anonymous workmen as well as Hollywood stars, another layer of fossilized history is superimposed on the ruins of the city. Those alive in the scene, then, are now as fossilized in their screen image as the plaster casts of the Pompeiian couple.

Various themes associated in different ways with death run throughout *Journey to Italy* and on the last day intrude more insistently on Alex and Katherine. There is the physical reality, the inevitability of death, that so upsets Katherine at Pompeii. And during the film the English couple encounter the Neapolitan culture surrounding death, both poignant and easy-going, assuming an afterlife and an intimacy between the living and the dead. This is not a culture of fear or, indeed, of the uncanny, and includes the broad beliefs of popular Catholicism, its statues, cults and miracles. In Freud's terms, this is a world in which 'primitive beliefs' are not yet 'surmounted'. For Rossellini, it represents a world that keeps alive the past through its ancient beliefs and through an easy everyday contact between the living, the present, and the dead, the past. This culture and its superstitions, the intermingling of past and present, lead to the cinema's fusion of past and present and its paradoxical capacity to preserve the living as inanimate ghosts, for which he finds allegorical representations throughout the film.

107

This cinema is a direct descendant of the 'natural magic' practised by Giacomo della Porta and Athanasius Kircher. For them, as for Rossellini, the machine's reality was a matter of both science and beauty.

Rossellini's films before 1952 prefigure his intense commitment to cinema's reality as well as his interest in the invisible, the remains of suffering, a lost past. Ruins come to have a privileged position as a metaphor for this meeting of material and immaterial worlds. His cinema was born during World War II and found maturity in the ruins left in its aftermath: the physically damaged cities and the mentally damaged people. The post-war films that established his international reputation, *Rome Open City* (1945) and *Paisà* (1946), were about Italy under occupation, very recent experiences that were still vivid in collective memory and Italian national consciousness. Rossellini chronicled the dramas and tragedies that overtake ordinary people caught in events beyond their control. The war was over but its reality was still visible and could be recorded before it faded into history. In *Germany Year Zero* (1947) and his first two films with Ingrid Bergman (*Stromboli*, 1949, *Europa 51*, 1952) the reality of war was in the marks left in the minds of people, the traumas that still persisted after the war and the occupation. From Rossellini's Catholic perspective, suffering marks the soul as it does the Freudian unconscious. From André Bazin onwards, critics have pointed out that Rossellini's cinema mediates between the visible and the invisible, whether in the translation of historical memory, the exteriorization of trauma or the materialization of the Christian soul. But he was particularly interested in the mingling of Catholicism and popular beliefs. *The Machine for Killing the Bad* (1948) is an explicit reflection on these interwoven worlds. The camera plays an explicitly central role, tying together the themes of superstition, popular Catholicism and, in a parody of photography, the transition from life to death. This film, set on the Amalfi coast that Rossellini associated so closely with popular religion, places the camera firmly within the legacy of the magical and the miraculous. When he came to make *Journey to Italy* in 1952, Rossellini was able to weave together these previous preoccupations and passions and bring the cinema's reality and its magic into dialogue with the popular culture of Naples and its environs.

The film begins with the Joyces driving in their Bentley through the Italian countryside, the open road signifying the opening of the story, its narrative line stretching towards Naples. The future blockages and delays to the story are prefigured as the Bentley is forced to slow its pace for some small herds of cattle. It is Alex's Uncle Homer's death that has brought them to Italy, to sell the house and property left to them. Forced to wait for prospective buyers, they find that Naples affects each of them differently and their marriage comes under increasing strain. Through the meandering middle section of the film, Alex and Katherine take the story into different directions. On the last day their paths re-converge. After the expedition to Pompeii, the film ends with the Joyces again in the Bentley, in a drive towards an end that balances the beginning. Again their path is halted by their surroundings, this time by a religious procession, dominated by a statue of the Madonna. This time, the halt precipitates their reconciliation and 'the end' on which narrative closure depends.

Journey to Italy was not an easy film to finance and Rossellini needed his stars Ingrid Bergman and George Sanders, from this practical point of view. But their presence gives an essential aesthetic weight to one side of Rossellini's experiment. As stars they are signifiers of Hollywood and represent a foil to the new kind of cinema that Rossellini introduced into the film. That is, without its stars, *Journey* would not have been able to symbolize so vividly a point of transition in cinema history. Rossellini left Bergman and Sanders without character guidelines or the usual support that serious actors expect from a serious director. As a result, as Rossellini intended, their presence on the screen is uncertain. Icons of stardom, they are also themselves, unsure where the boundary lies between performing stardom, performing as actors or as stars who are forced to perform themselves. However, within the fiction, the characters of Alex and Katherine Joyce enable the film to create an opposition between different kinds of cinemas, divided between modern and conventional modes of cinematic story-telling. Katherine carves out a space for reflection and for the journey into the past. Alex is impatient to drive the action forward. Katherine allows the plot to wander. Alex tries to keep it on track with an ordered sense of movement and event. These divergent directions divide along gender lines, with masculinity and its anxieties identified with conventional action-driven narrative and femininity with the kind of cinema that would enable Rossellini's 'essay', that is, his journey to Naples and its past.

In this experiment with film narrative, Alex and Katherine Joyce represent divergent paths not only due to gender but also due to the opposing but emblematic attitudes to time. Through Alex, Rossellini introduces the geographical difference between northern and southern culture and *mores* (implicit also between north and south Italy). The ordered clock time of the north encounters uneasily the more leisured time of the south, just as the smooth forward path of the Bentley had been halted by the cattle. After their first lunch at Uncle Homer's house, on the second day, Alex and Katherine lie in the winter sun on the terrace. Here the tensions in their marriage and the directions in which they will take the story begin to come to the surface. Alex is restless. The empty time of the siesta begins to bore him and he wanders off in search of more wine, taking the story into one of its small digressions. He wanders downstairs into the kitchen and wakes the sleeping servants; then a series of linguistic misunderstandings leads to his increasing discomfiture. This is a north–south confrontation but also one of sex and class as the representative of the north, bourgeois and male, faces the representative of the south, working-class, female and woken from her siesta.

On the terrace, Katherine has been daydreaming in a mental journey of her own, into her past and her relationship with Charles Lewington, a poet who had been in love with her and had died after the war. He had been in Naples with the British Army and Katherine associates the city with him and his poetry. As she tells Alex the story, eyes closed and half-asleep, this lapse into a 'feminine' world of poetry and sentiment irritates him profoundly and provokes an irrational outburst of jealousy. This episode is based on the central premise of James Joyce's story 'The Dead'.[6] Katherine's relationship with the young poet echoes Gretta's with Michael Furey. Both women have been loved hopelessly by a young, sensitive and frail man, one a singer, the other a poet, who then die prematurely. In both cases, this young, doomed, long-dead lover returns by a chance triggering of memory to disrupt the present. But once felt, his presence haunts both husbands. In 'The Dead', jealousy and irritation give way to an intimation of universal mortality; in *Journey*, Alex's jealousy exacerbates his impatience, his sense of impotence, his irritation with Katherine. Charles Lewington haunts Katherine, Alex and the film itself.[7] Katherine's memory first introduces this 'ghost', but Alex's jealousy keeps him there, an eruption of the past into the present. But other ghosts haunt the film. For instance, Uncle Homer's aristocratic Neapolitan friends not only joke about his death but talk easily of meeting him 'up there', as though exchange between the living and the dead were commonplace. Charles drives a wedge between Alex and Katherine, but his ghostly presence in the Joyces' rational world creates a link to the part played by 'the dead' in Neapolitan popular culture.

The growing distance between Alex and Katherine during the empty waiting time sends the story into a series of loops, small journeys of thematic rather than narrative significance. For Gilles Deleuze, Rossellini's cinema, along with other significant directors of Italian Neo-realism, marks a point of transition between the 'movement image' and the 'time image'. D. N. Rodowick sums up the change:

> According to Deleuze, the appearance of neo-realism represents a crisis in the cinema of action and movement. Especially in Rossellini's films, such as *Germania Anno Zero* (1947) and *Stromboli* (1949) or *Viaggio in Italia* (1953), narrative situations appear where reality is represented as lacunary and dispersive. Linear actions dissolve into aleatory strolls. Events occur where it is no longer possible to act or react . . . Since the linking of motor

images is no longer activated by action, space changes in nature, becoming a disconnected or empty space. Acts of seeing or hearing replace the linking of images through motor actions; pure description replaces referential anchoring.[8]

Alex's part, played perfectly by George Sanders, is to rebel against this decline of action and the change of pace. Empty space and time bore him as though he were a reluctant spectator of a Neo-realist movie. He stands for the cinema of 'movement image', and for a defensive desire for action and order that masks his fear of impotence and loss of masculinity. For Alex there is something demasculinizing about southern time and his recurring rant against the 'laziness' of Naples is, on some level, a complaint about the plot, its lack of energy and direction.[9] Given the irony that Rossellini invests in the characterizations of Alex and Katherine, his mischievous blurring of the boundaries between fiction and reality, there is also an element of complaint about the director himself and his refusal to play by the rules of the 'movement image'. All the plot offers Alex in the way of action or event is a small opportunity for sexual adventure. On the fifth day he follows his pleasure-loving friends, particularly Marie, to Capri. Once again, nothing happens and Alex loses another round in his struggle with the meandering plot. His attempt to bring action, even sexual action, to the story fails miserably. His search for an adventure tails away to impotence as Marie quite simply rejects him.

Katherine, on the other hand, guides the film willingly into highly determined, mythical spaces in which her role is to look into the past and link its sites to the wider terrain of the film's themes. It is hard to describe Katherine's journeys as feminine in any particularly positive way, except in the sense that the woman, by tradition and convention, has had less control over the cinema's 'action image' than her male equivalent. A female guide is neutral rather than feminine; her passivity more easily allows other kinds of narrative time and space to materialize in her presence. In his characterization of Katherine, Rossellini shows a sneaking sympathy for Alex's irritation with her rather smug sentimentality and her caricature get-up as English lady tourist, as well as for Alex's preference for having 'fun' in Capri over visiting museums ('museums bore me').

The stars' performances confirm that Rossellini intended to produce reality, not realism, in *Journey to Italy*. Bergman and Sanders had no script and the schedule seemed chaotic, offering little by way of clues to chronology of event or emotional structure. Essentially they were expected to be spontaneous, improvise and play themselves. The traditions and conventions of star- and event-driven cinema are overtaken by the emptiness that allows another kind of cinema to feel its way into being. When the journey's narrative momentum comes to a halt, time opens up for digression and reflection so that this new cinema seems to be coming into being before one's eyes. In this sense, the film allows time not only for thought about its themes, but also for thought about the cinema and its history. The presence of disorientated Hollywood stars in a European art film dramatizes such a change in cinematic direction. And perhaps the only Hollywood stars who would have been prepared to participate in, and thus enable, this crisis in the narrative film would be these two semi-Europeans, both at crisis points in their lives, both uncertain as to where their private and professional futures were leading. In *Journey to Italy*, out of a minimal plot line and two bewildered Hollywood stars, Rossellini managed to create, in the opinion of many critics, the first modern film. At the same time, he replaces realism, a style of cinematic fiction, with reality, documenting places and people, passers-by in the street, as well as his stars. The fictional journey undertaken by Alex and Katherine Joyce is partially pushed to the side by history, geography and geology.

Almost like a refrain running throughout the film, Rossellini punctuates *Journey* with sweeping panning shots which take in the expanse of the Bay of Naples. These shots descend directly from the visual culture of nineteenth-century Naples, which celebrated the bay's beauty and its status as a tourist attraction. Giuliana Bruno describes this tradition:

> Attention to panoramas, exterior views and landscape is traditionally
> an important component of the visual culture of Naples . . . This is
> reflected in its artistic tradition: landscapes and 'vedute' [views] pre-
> dominate in Italian art from painting to photography.[10]

The Joyces' first morning in Naples opens with a pan of the whole
bay, accompanied by a Neapolitan folk song, taken from their window but detached from their point of view. The second pan is
from Uncle Homer's terrace. As Tony, his manager, points out the
features of the landscape to Alex and Katherine, the whole expanse
of the bay is mapped out. The camera follows his gestures:

> Over there is the Vesuvius, ever since the eruption of 1944 there has
> been a period of calm but the temperature is beginning to rise a little
> though. That point there, behind the hill, that first hill, is Pompeii.
> Then Castellammare, Torre Annunziata. Resina's over there and
> Naples. There's Ischia, the Isle of Capri and that large strip down
> there is the Sorrento peninsula.

Vesuvius dominates the landscape physically and also dominates the culture that the film explores, the relation between the
material relics of the past and the symptoms of religious belief. The
volcano is a geological phenomenon that has created a specific geographical environment. The rich volcanic soil produced a thriving
agricultural economy, and an eruption created the natural harbour
and the curve of the bay that first established the strategic significance of Naples in the ancient world. The rich history of the area
grew out of the natural conditions created by the volcano. The
Greek colony of Parthenope and Neapolis, with foundations at
Cumae dating back to about 750 BC, became the most flourishing
economic and intellectual community outside Greece. Later,
Roman intellectuals, such as Virgil, were drawn to the Greek
culture that continued to flourish in the city after the decline of
Athenian power. The beautiful coast, islands and volcanic baths
have made a playground for the rich from ancient times, bringing
wealth and culture to the area. The Roman emperors Tiberius,

Nero and Caligula built themselves luxurious villas on Capri and Ischia, initiating the islands' long-standing, if later less excessive, association with decadence. The towns of Pompeii and Herculaneum grew up on the mainland as the Roman rich, attracted to the sea bathing, the volcanic hot springs and mineral waters, turned the bay area into the first European holiday resort during the first century AD. The traces of this history are there in the sites that feature so prominently in *Journey to Italy*.

But the volcano has its other side. In AD 79 came the eruption that destroyed Pompeii and Herculaneum as Vesuvius revealed its dark and destructive power. The population, tied to the economic benefits and the pleasures of the volcanic landscape, lived in perpetual fear of Vesuvius, and an array of cults and superstitions has always been rife in its environs. This tradition, already characteristic of the daily life of Pompeii, continued in the semi-pagan, semi-Catholic religion, with its ritual processions and statues of saints that fascinated Rossellini. Vesuvius illustrates vividly the way that a material, geographical, reality creates cultural practice and religious belief. The most significant symbol of Neapolitan popular culture is missing from *Journey to Italy*: the patron saint of Naples, San Gennaro. Since the fourteenth century, San Gennaro has been the Neapolitan antidote to Vesuvius. Three times a year the saint's blood miraculously liquefies, defending Naples from all kinds of harm, but most particularly from the volcano. Tag Gallagher's biography of Rossellini reproduces the roughly written list of locations, the city's historic sites that were to be included in the film.[11] Three locations are not in the final film, and the most important of these is the Cappella di San Gennaro, in Naples Cathedral.

Discussing his fascination with Neapolitan popular culture in a *Cahiers du Cinéma* interview in 1954, Rossellini mentions San Gennaro, saying:

> Besides, you must remember that Naples is the only place in the world where a miracle takes place on a fixed date, September 19th, the miracle of San Gennaro. And San Gennaro look out! If the

miracle doesn't happen, he gets into trouble. And all kinds of dreadful things start to happen![12]

But no sequence relating to this central figure was filmed. Probably the chapel of San Gennaro was too holy and his cult too sacred for filming to have been allowed in the cathedral.[13] But the miracle relates closely to the themes that interested Rossellini. The liquefaction of the dead saint's blood pre-empts the coming to life of the volcano, or, if the worst comes to the worst, stills the invading flow of molten lava. Both these phenomena, the natural and the superstitious, revolve around movement and stillness, the animation of an inanimate substance and lead to the culture of the uncanny.

Although San Gennaro is missing, Katherine's sightseeing trips take the film to sites that have a related significance. Her first journey, on the third day, is to the Archaeological Museum of Naples. This sequence is not a record of a tourist's visit but a careful selection of images that are relevant to Rossellini's 'essay' film. In this large and complex museum, he decided to concentrate on only a few of the statues. The sequence is filmed with an extremely mobile camera, a crane and tracks, which was necessary not only to film in proportion to the size of the enormous Farnese statues,[14] but also to give the sequence its distinctive style. The camera movements take on their own autonomy, moving beyond Katherine's point of view, enhanced by the first appearance of Renzo Rossellini's music. As Katherine and the guide reach the Farnese *Hercules*, the camera moves higher with sweeping movements, defying gravity as it transcends the limitations of the human eye and its earthbound perspective. Throughout the sequence the music, with its eerie, other-worldly quality, is mixed in ironic juxtaposition to the guide's patter.

Rossellini begins the sequence with a dissolve that brings Katherine into the museum as it were through the huge stone base of a pillar. Movement emerges out of stasis, setting the scene for the rest of the sequence. It is as though Rossellini imagined that his camera would be the magic means of bringing life to those blocks of stone. Most of the statues are poised in mid-gesture, the

Discus Thrower with his eyes looking just above the camera, the *Drunken Poet* caught at the moment he falls backwards into a stupor. It is as though the gaze of the Medusa, or some other malign magician, had turned living movement into stone. Classical Greek sculpture, later copied by the Romans, aspired to create the illusion of a frozen moment. Rossellini's concentration on this style creates a link that jumps across the centuries to photography's transformation of this aspiration into reality and to André Bazin's sweeping condensation of the history of art into this single line of progression. In *Journey*, however, the camera adds a dimension that transcends still photography, as it brings the cinema's movement to the statues, attempting to reanimate their stillness. This strategy reaches a crescendo with the gigantic Farnese *Bull* group, in which the brothers, Zethus and Amphion, struggle to hold still the huge rearing bull on which Dirce, who lies at their feet, will be tied. The camera circles around this violent scene, both extending its melodramatic, theatrical qualities and trying to duplicate the sculptor's attempt to create the appearance of an action caught at that split second and then left for ever in suspended animation. Rossellini celebrates the way these sculptures convey movement in stillness, images of life in inanimate stone.

Katherine's visit to Cumae, on day five, presents a sharp contrast to the aesthetic of the statues in the Museum. The statues belong to a comparatively short and historically coherent period of ancient history. Cumae's history is layered with different epochs, different cultures, different religions and mythologies. The oldest of the Greek settlements, with its massive walls supposedly in Minoan style, Cumae stretches back into prehistory and emerges into mythology as the site of the Sibyl's cave. After the decline of Rome, the Christians used the site as catacombs and later the Saracens used it as a fortress. In contrast to the museum, the sequence is organized around Katherine's subjective responses to the place. The guide, telescoping the long history of the site, says: 'After abandoning Troy, Aeneas landed here on this very beach. In the last war, the British troops landed here.' The subsequent shot shows Katherine's reaction as it dawns on her that Charles

Lewington had probably encamped in that very spot. The guide demonstrates the echo that resounds through the huge passage and Rossellini holds the shot of Katherine and the guide walking, with light and shadow falling across their path, until they reach a chamber of Christian remains. The music links the scene back to the eerie atmosphere of the museum. The lines of Charles's poem begin to run through Katherine's head, but the guide breaks into her reverie, drawing her attention to two marks on the wall where, he claims, the Saracens chained their prisoners: 'This is how they would have tied a beautiful woman like you.'

Although its uncanniness is, by and large, refracted through Katherine's thoughts and Charles's ghostly presence, Cumae brings with it an accumulation of resonance, trace and relic. It is also a place of mystery, or rather of 'the mysteries', the secrets of the religion, whether of the Oracle or of early Christianity, that their devotees believed in. The echo, which takes on a life of its own as it reverberates, accentuates that aura of dematerialized mystery. At the same time, the echo is also a material link with the past, in continuity with all the previous echoes, stretching back across the centuries to when, as the guide explains, it was much louder because the walls were covered in bronze. And, bringing the atmosphere of the scene out of its other-worldliness into its historical reality, Rossellini uses the marks made on the wall by the pirates as a material sign of the presence of the past, an indexical inscription.

Katherine's third journey, on day six, takes her to the Phlegraean Fields, where she witnesses the live volcanic activity of the 'little Vesuvius' and the 'mystery' of ionization. Here the film reaches into the seething substructure of the area that occasionally comes to the surface, as in these sulphur pits or in the actual eruptions of Vesuvius itself. The sequence is organized visually in two contrasting ways. On the one hand, there is Katherine's delight in the natural phenomena she is witnessing. She photographs the smoking pits, experiments with the ionization mystery, exclaiming as the whole area responds in unison to one lighted paper or cigarette with a massive increase in smoke. She recognizes, in the 'pocket Vesuvius', the ash and cinders that had buried Pompeii in AD 79. Meanwhile, the camera finds its own independent relation with the movement of the smoke. As the volume of smoke increases, the camera follows it as it drifts away until it fills the screen. There is a stark contrast between the camera's relation to the hard-edged, exquisitely worked bodies in the museum and this insubstantial flow without shape or form, beginning or end. As the smoke drifts across the screen and the camera drifts with it, once again, even if on a less formally evolved level, the image moves away from its fictional frame of reference. Film turns into something beyond its usual subservience to iconic representation, dissolving into wispy grey tones. But there is a thematic link back to the two previous expeditions. The volcanic activity and the smoke from the ionization process have a flow and a movement that animate an inanimate material, the earth itself.

Katherine leads the plot to one side of her own fictional story, standing back, as it were, to allow the cinema to find its own dialogue with the history and geography of the area so that Rossellini can extract and translate into film the visible presence of the past. The statues, frozen in motion, have an analogous relation to photography, preserving the stilled movement of the human body 'then' across time into 'now'. Cumae, on the other hand, is topography and exists across time. A sacred site since prehistory due to its intrinsic geomantic qualities, it was subsequently overlaid by layers of other histories that add to the power of the place itself. While the statues are like snapshots, moments of frozen time, Cumae is a palimpsest. As a place sanctified by human belief in the supernatural, it leads logically to the sulphur pits, where a natural phenomenon assumes the appearance of mystery. The theme that unifies the three sites, on a second level, is the relation between inanimate matter and its animation. The statues, still and inorganic, aspire to depict human movement, gesture and a moment of time so that the inanimate and inorganic masquerade as organic and animate. Cumae's walls come alive with the echo of voices, reaching back across time to the haunting presence of spirits and ghosts summoned up by the power of human belief. Most particularly, the volcano challenges the separation of movement and stillness into the organic and the inorganic. All three relate to the mysteriousness of the cinema in which inanimate photograms come alive in projection, giving frozen moments of time a semblance of animation.

Towards the end of the film both Alex and Katherine encounter a more immediate presence of death as a faint trace left by the suffering of World War II. Alex meets a young prostitute who has just witnessed the death of her best friend and has, herself, only a residual wish to live. Although this is not ultimately a sexual encounter, it evokes the memory of Naples under the occupation when so many women were reduced to prostitution in the face of starvation. This episode is the only scene that harks back to *Paisà*, a film made just seven years earlier. For Katherine, the encounter is more vivid.

The Joyces' hostess, Natalia, offers to take Katherine to the Church of the Fontanelle, in which skulls and skeletons are piled around the walls. Rossellini tells an anecdote in his autobiography about the Neapolitan attitude to the dead. When an influx of people from the country overwhelmed the city in the nineteenth century, the skeletons of the dead were displaced from the graveyards, which were then deconsecrated to make room for living people. The bones were thrown into the Roman catacombs. When the poor hid in the catacombs during World War II families gradually began to adopt individual skeletons. He says:

> I was told 'We have lost so many sons on the other side of the sea. No one knows where they're buried, dispersed by the wind and the sand or burnt by the . . . sun. We have nothing, not a tomb, not a cross to pray to. So we have turned to these; they will stand for our loved ones in front of God.'[15]

In the church, Natalia tells Katherine about her brother who was killed somewhere in Greece and whom she mourns in this church of the unburied. Katherine is disturbed by the skulls and skeletons and she watches Natalia from a distance as she makes the, to Katherine, unfamiliar gestures of the Catholic faith.

The skeletons: Church of the Fontanelle.

In *Journey to Italy* reality constantly intrudes into the fiction. These tensions come to the fore at the end of the film. Alex and Katherine are driving from Pompeii when a religious procession in a small town on the Amalfi coast halts the progress of the Bentley.[16] Just as the film had opened with the visual equivalent of a play on the word 'drive', so narrative closure also finds a graphic visualization in the car's gradual loss of speed, for the word 'end'. There is an application of the brakes, a blocked passage. Now Rossellini weaves together two endings. Alex and Katherine are forced to leave the car at the moment when a cry of 'miracle' comes from the procession as a cripple throws away his crutches in front of the Madonna. Katherine is dragged away by the press of people rushing forward. As Alex and Katherine find each other again, the miracle of the cure is repeated in the miracle of the conventional happy end, essential both to Hollywood and to folk-tales, the *deus ex machina* that enables the forward drive of narrative to find stasis. In recognition of this convention, Alex and Katherine declare their love and they kiss in the time-honoured image of cinematic narrative closure.

But this ending does not fit Rossellini's concept of cinema. The camera turns away from the star couple and their ending. A crane shot follows the people streaming along the street; and the camera then finds its own ending in this renewed flow of movement, not of narrative but of reality. The film simply fades away

The Hollywood ending.

Life goes on.

as the local brass band plays and people drift past. Life goes on. One ending halts, the other flows. One is a concentration focused on the stars' role in producing the fiction and its coherence, and the other is a distraction, the film's tendency to wander off in search of another kind of cinema. This is the 'continuance of time' that, for Jacques Rivette, is the essential element in Rossellini's mode of story-telling.

Chapter Seven

Abbas Kiarostami: Cinema of Uncertainty, Cinema of Delay

In *A Taste of Cherry* (1997) Kiarostami combines the story of his protagonist's search for death with the mobile cinematic style that he had developed in his two previous films, *Where is my Friend's House?* (1987) and *And Life Goes On* (1991). Shooting from a car, the camera's movement delineates the movement of the journey to create a fusion between the cinema's movement, a narrative's movement towards its end and the inevitable end of life. Here the topography of the death drive is unlike the horizontal direction of the drive in the 'dying together' B movies, or Marion's unconscious drive towards death in the first section of *Psycho*. The journey moves in wide circular sweeps through the landscape, returning from time to time to the place that the driver has selected for his grave. Mr Badiei has decided to commit suicide. He is willing to pay someone a large sum of money to come to his grave the following morning, confirm his death and bury his body. His attempts to persuade three very different men to agree to his proposal break up the film's narrative direction into a series of encounters, all taking place in his car. The first, a Kurdish soldier, jumps out of the car and runs away in horror when the driver stops to show him the grave. The second, an Afghan seminarian, tries to dissuade Badiei, arguing that suicide is a sin. The third, an older man who works as a taxidermist, at first tries to dissuade him, arguing that life is worth living for its small pleasures, such as the taste of the cherry. But in the last resort he agrees to help him on the grounds that the choice between life and death is a natural right.

Finally, 'the end' is represented metaphorically through the different allegorical levels of the story, narrative structure and cinema. When Mr Badiei reaches his grave, the screen shows the night sky with a storm coming up. The moon goes behind the clouds and the screen fades and remains black. 'One is aware that there is nothing there', says Kiarostami. 'But life comes from light. Here, cinema and life merge into one another. Because the cinema, too, is only light. . . The spectator has to confront this non-existence which, for me, evokes a symbolic death.'[1] After the black screen, representing the end of life, narrative and cinema, a short coda undermines the finality of this ending. Shot on video, the grainy image shows the landscape transformed into the fertile green of spring. The film crew are at work; Homayoon Irshadi, who plays Mr Badiei, lights a cigarette; the soldiers are resting by the roadside. While the theme of death demands finality, an ending in the manner of Hitchcock, Kiarostami ends the film more in the spirit of Rossellini and *Journey to Italy*, where, after its formal end, the film casually indicates that life goes on. However, Louis Armstrong's 'St James' Infirmary' plays on the sound-track accompanying the coda sequence. The song simply, in two verses, tells of a man who finds his lover laid out dead in the morgue and who then visualizes his own death. While the sequence undermines the death-drive ending, it acknowledges the film's production. The symbolic death of Kiarostami then announces that the shoot is over.

The thematic preoccupations and the style of *A Taste of Cherry* are concentrated into distilled form and the film is one of Kiarostami's most abstract. Peter Brooks comments on the significance of repetition in narratives of the death drive. Repetition in the text holds back its forward movement, postponing or delaying the end. He points out that the line of narrative cannot follow the straightest path from point to point without deviating from its course. 'The shortest distance between beginning and end would be the collapse of one into the other, of life into immediate death.'[2] The narrative form into which the principle of delay translates may vary significantly, built around, for instance, an aesthetic of suspense or, at a further extreme, the intrusion of digression or the

Where is my Friend's House?.
Ahmed and Mohammed (the
Ahmedapour brothers) at school
(*Khaneh-ye dust kojast?*, 1987).

'aleatory strolls' that Gilles Deleuze associates with the loosening of the movement image, as, for instance, in Rossellini's *Journey to Italy*. In Kiarostami's cinema, an aesthetic of digression leads towards an aesthetic of reality, not in a simple opposition to fiction, but towards ways in which the cinema acknowledges the limitations of representation. In the Koker trilogy, shot between 1987 and 1994, Kiarostami twice went back over a previous work and attempted to mobilize a cinema of observation that would follow absences in representation that are usually displaced by the needs of an externally determined system of ordering, such as narrational coherence.

Abbas Kiarostami was overtaken in 1990 by a real and traumatic event that directly affected his cinema. In 1987 he had made *Where is my Friend's House?*, which in 1989 won the Bronze Leopard at the Locarno Film Festival. The film takes place in the villages of Koker and Potesh, several hundred miles to the north of Tehran, and tells the story of a boy, Ahmed (Babek Ahmedapour), about ten years old, who realizes that his friend Mohammed Nematzadeh (Ahmed Ahmedapour) has dropped his exercise book after school. Because he will not be able to do his homework, Mohammed will be punished the next day by the teacher, so Ahmed sets out from Koker to Potesh to return the exercise book and find the house of his friend. No one he encounters seems able to, or is prepared to, help him. It begins to get dark and, as Ahmed begins to feel nervous, a horse's sudden appearance out of the shadows brings his fear to the surface. An old man rather ineffectu-

125

Ahmed's journey.

ally befriends him. When Ahmed gets home, he completes both his own and his friend's homework, which the teacher then approves at school the next day.

Everyone acting in the film came from the villages and the film was an elaboration on the themes that Kiarostami had been developing for some years in his commissions from the Committee for the Education of Children and Young Adults. The film continues to dramatize the importance of children within the post-Revolution era and draws attention to the significance of education in creating a new, articulate and socially aware generation. Kiarostami's films from this period also draw attention to children's oppression. In a society in which parents and teachers alike had traditionally tended to treat them with mixed indifference and cruelty, children had to be given a voice and a point of view.

In 1990, after the film had become Kiarostami's first international success, an appalling earthquake hit the area in which *Where is my Friend's House?* had been filmed. Many lives were lost; the agricultural economy was devastated; and the peasants from the ruined villages had to live in improvised camps near the main roads where they could at least receive relief from outside. In *And Life Goes On* (1991) Farhad Kherdamand, a friend of Kiarostami's, plays the 'director' of *Where is my Friend's House?* who hears of the disaster at home in Tehran and returns to the area, accompanied by his own little boy Puya (played by the son of the cinematographer). During the course of the day, they try to get to Koker, via roads blocked by chaotic traffic or by taking detours along side roads, to find out whether or not the Ahmedapour brothers had survived. Echoing the previous film, the story starts out as a journey with a quest, with the original search for a friend and his house transposed to the quest for the boys themselves. Farhad and Puya show people the film poster depicting the boys to help identify them. In the earthquake zone, the camera tracks from the moving car along stretches of road lined with ruined houses and ruined lives. People dig through the rubble, try to save a few possessions or take in the tragedy that has hit them. The film pauses to register and record these scenes of complete devastation, death and loss and people stunned by the earthquake: 'It attacked like a hungry wolf, killing all it could reach', 'Only ruins and misery left'. People of all ages recount the numbers lost in their families, strange stories of their own survival, and speculate about God's responsibility for the disaster. The director, Farhad, looks from the car window at the devastated lives around him and there is a suggestion that a future film, bearing witness to the suffering and courage of these people, is beginning to take shape in his mind. It is at this point that the film begins to face in two different directions. With the search for the boys and a chance meeting with Mr Ruhi, who had played the old man who tried to help Ahmed in *Where is my Friend's House?*, this film, *And Life Goes On,* looks back to the past, but the director's experiences and encounters also lead to the future, to the third film of the trilogy. *Through the Olive Trees* (1994) will be about the filming of a drama-documentary that reconstructs episodes taken from Farhad's journey into the aftermath of the earthquake. Farhad Kherdamand will still play the original 'director' of *Where is my Friend's House?*, and will participate in the re-enactment of scenes that he had witnessed in *And Life Goes On*. But his part will be a minor one, replaced by another representative of the role 'director', an actor playing the director of the drama-documentary. In the first shot of *Through the Olive Trees* a man introduces himself, speaking directly to camera: 'I am Mohammed Ali Keshavarz. I am the actor who plays the director. The other actors were all hired on location.' But as the filming of the drama-documentary continues, its attempt to recreate the trauma of the past will be displaced by another story, which will gradually emerge to pose another problem of representation and narration.

And Life Goes On mediates between the first and the third of the Koker trilogy not only chronologically, charting the impact of the earthquake, but also in terms of the earthquake's impact on Kiarostami's cinema in relation to reality and its representation. One recurring theme of the film is the gap separating the reality of a traumatic event and any attempt to turn it into an exegesis, a representational account of the event. Kiarostami introduces various narrative devices to make this point, the first being to separate the devastation as filmed from the original traumatic moment of the disaster itself. Commenting on the encounter between the director and his son with Mr Ruhi, Kiarostami says: 'I quite simply wanted to remind the spectators, in the middle of the screening, that they were watching a film and not reality. Because reality – that is the moment when the earthquake happened – we were not there to film.'3

This gap between the event and the later filming was unavoidable, but instead of attempting to close it, Kiarostami acknowledges the distance between a reality and its representation. Delay here is not only a fact but also a factor in the film's aesthetic. There is a correlation between this aesthetic and the relationship between trauma and exegesis in psychoanalysis. Lacan's category of 'the Real' refers to the actuality of a traumatic event, personal or historical. The mind searches for words or images that might translate and convey that reality. But its translation into 'Symbolic' form and into consciousness separates the two, just as an account of a dream is separated from the time of dreaming and loses its original feeling. Faced with the reality of the tragedy, the film tries to find ways of translating it. The search for the two boys is delayed by blocked roads, and the repeated stories of tragedy and survival actually force the film to slow down to a stop as it tries to register and inscribe the transition between disaster and the way that 'life goes on'. Death, not just in terms of the scale of this tragedy, creates a link between the aesthetic and the psychoanalytic, representing an ultimate 'unspeakable', beyond conscious comprehension, the source of the rituals, cultural phenomena and belief systems that attempt to make sense of it.

This pause in the narrative, its delay among the ruins, recalls Deleuze's vision of a cinema of the time-image emerging out of the ruins of World War II. Italian Neo-realism reflected the shock left by the war and the need for a new cinematic way of thinking about the world. The shock demanded, in Deleuze's terms, the weakening of the 'sensory-motor situation'. That is, a film aesthetic derived from the logic of action, fuelled and duplicated by the cinema's forward drive into movement, would start to hesitate and find ways of responding to its surroundings, deriving images from whatever the camera observed rather than a narrative aspiration to order and organization. With the decline of action, an evacuated cinematic space fills the gap, registering the empty images of landscape or cityscape that Deleuze associates with the post-war cinema of Rossellini. This cinema of record, observation and delay tends to work with elongated shots, enabling the presence of time to appear on the screen. The duration of the shots draws attention to time as it passes on the screen, the film's present, but the lack of action confronts the audience with a palpable sense of cinematic time that leads back, from the time of screening, to the time of registration, the past. While this delay is built into technology (cinematic time is always out of kilter), this sense of the past may find a complement in content. The past in the form of traces and ruins fills the content of the image in the cinema of Rossellini and in these films of Kiarostami. For Deleuze, this cinema demands a character who observes the scene, a 'seer', standing aside from action or narrative event:

These are pure optical and sound situations, in which the character does not know how to respond, abandoned spaces in which he ceases to experience and to act so that he enters into flight, goes on a trip, comes and goes, vaguely indifferent as to what happens to him, undecided as to what must be done. But he has gained the ability to see what he has lost in action or reaction: he SEES so that the viewer's problem becomes 'What is there to see in the image?' (and not now 'What are we going to see in the next image?').[4]

And Life Goes On conforms to this pattern.

Kiarostami, in common with many of his generation, had been influenced by Italian Neo-realism,[5] and his previous films, including *Where is my Friend's House?*, had been shot within the Iranian reworking of a realist aesthetic. The shock of the earthquake and its aftermath redirected Kiarostami's realism towards the difficult question of a reality that challenged adequate representation. With *And Life Goes On*, he introduces a 'seer' into the story. Farhad fulfils this function but also acts 'the director' whose role is to translate what he sees into cinema. The movement image, the drive of narrative, is put on pause not so much by an aesthetic crisis but by shock. The sight of such chaos and devastation delays the journey, breaking it up into episodes and short encounters that allow people to tell their stories. Editing is no longer smooth. Tracking shots from the slow-moving car have the integrity or self-sufficiency of the long take and often have little regard for correct, directional, continuity editing. This kind of shooting style conforms to André Bazin's view that the long take opens up time for thought within the flow of film. He argues that composition in depth, shots that avoid editing and maintain a unity of time and space, 'affect the relationship of the minds of the spectators to the image', implying:

> a more active mental attitude on the part of the spectator and a more positive contribution on his part to the action in progress . . . here is called on to exercise at least a minimum of personal choice. It is from his attention and his will that the meaning of the image in part derives.[6]

Bazin identifies Italian Neo-realism's investment in the continuum and 'ambiguity of reality' as the formative moment in which this cinema developed.

Early in *And Life Goes On*, with a long tracking shot along a grove of olive trees, the film first seems to indicate a loss of direction, distracted from the search for the boys and even from the aftermath of the earthquake. The camera is absorbed by the dappled light and shade that seem to dance as the wind moves through the trees. But the end of the shot breaks the spell of the landscape and returns to the suffering of the people trying to live in it. As the director stops the car and walks into the olive grove, he hears the sound of crying and finds a baby, quite alone, lying in a little hammock hung between two trees. He tries to comfort it until his own son starts calling for him; as he leaves, the mother appears in the distance collecting firewood. This is one of the encounters that will be reconstructed in *Through the Olive Trees*. It is also the first of many shots, in both films, that record, again with long tracking shots, the movement of wind through trees. While these shots are a meditation on the relation between movement and light and shade, in the cinema and natural landscape, even as they create a contrast to the scenes of devastation, they are also a reminder that the earthquake itself was an act of nature. Like the volcano in *Journey to Italy*, the earthquake represents the sudden eruption into movement of something that should have remained still and the sudden transformation of a benevolent nature into a vengeful and destructive force. The recurring shots of trees blowing in the wind seem to suggest the presence of some animistic force giving a kind of personification to the victims' reflections on the source of the disaster, God or nature: 'It was God's will' or 'No, this wasn't God's doing'.

In *Through the Olive Trees* the two 'directors', Farhad, now acting in the drama-documentary, and its fictional director, the actor Mohammed, are walking together in the early morning, looking out from the meadow where the film crew have camped, to the ruined village on the opposite hill. The presence of these 'directors' on the screen substantiates the gap in time, the delay, that separates an event and its representation, its process of translation in thought and creativity. As if to embody further the idea of separation and delay, the two men are discussing the echo that comes from the ruined village and the legend that its former inhabitants mysteriously answer a shouted greeting. This extends the natural phenomenon of the echo as a form of delay to its more ghostly connotations, voices from the past echoing across time and the boundary between the living and the dead. Farhad's attempt to try out the echo actually summons up the voice of Puya, his fictional son in *And Life Goes On*, who returns his call from, as it were, the previous film. As the scene ends and Farhad turns away to go back to the camp, he gives a sudden start as though touched by something invisible. These slight intimations of the uncanny lead to an emblematic and prolonged tracking shot of the wind in the olive trees.

The cinematic style in *And Life Goes On* is marked by the graphic presence of the road, as a visual motif but also as the means by which aid and supplies can reach the people. These elongated sequences of driving, the long tracking shots taken from a moving car, subsequently came to be a hallmark of Kiarostami's cinema. Journeys, actual and metaphoric, had always been a recurring narrative theme in his films, from the early short *The Bread and Alley* (in which a small boy has to get through an alley occupied by a dog) to Ahmed's journey from Koker to Potesh. With the return to Koker, it is as though the uncertainty that the earthquake had brought to the already difficult lives of the peasants has to be reflected in cinema's own loss of certainty. The comparative certainty of realism weakens as it struggles to find its way to create a visual record of an actual historical tragedy, and the cinema begins to materialize in the gap separating the event and its adequate representation. In this case, the car forms a pivotal point between recurrent shots of its movement along the road and the camera's elongated movements across the landscape. These shots combine an image of a forward direction for the journey that, since it is not filled by characterization or fiction, demands thought or wonder, with a camera that observes the actions of characters and story. But when the film does encounter people on its journey, its search for the boys and the reiterated presence of the previous film act as reminders of the uncertain status of events shown on the screen.

The presence of a surrogate 'seer', which Deleuze associates with the time-image, is embodied in the character of the 'director'.

After the tragedy of the earthquake, the relations between the director and the local people, invisible in *Where is my Friend's House?*, have to become the subject of observation and comment; a surrogate director has to appear on the screen to represent the distortion and loss that accompany any cinematic record of reality. Kiarostami implies that not only were they not there to film the earthquake, but that the trauma demands a new recognition of the gap between urban, middle-class film-maker and the reality of shattered lives. The film can bear witness to these lives, but it cannot represent their truth. The first sign of the break between the first film of the trilogy and the aftermath of the earthquake in *And Life Goes On* takes the form of a retrospective 'self-critique'. Farhad and Puya overtake Mr Ruhi as he trudges along the road carrying a toilet. They give him a lift in the car to his house and a conversation ensues about the part he had played in the previous film. Puya says he had appeared to be much older in the film. Mr Ruhi answers:

> These gentlemen told me I should look older . . . they made me wear a hump to look older. The truth is, I didn't like it. I said 'Yes sir. Whatever you say sir.' They were cruel to me. I don't know what kind of art it is that shows people older and uglier. It's strange . . .

When they arrive at the house, the conversation continues:

> Puya: I expected to see you in the same house as before . . .
> Mr Ruhi: That was my film house. It wasn't my real home. The truth is this isn't my real one either. This, too, is my film house. The gentlemen said 'Let this be your house.' But the truth is that my house was destroyed in the earthquake. I'm living in a tent for now.

He then tries to find a bowl with which to give Puya a drink of water, as laid down in the script, but the balcony doors are locked and he is unable to locate the right prop. He calls out towards the camera for help and Miss Rabbi, the script girl, runs on set to give it to him. This is the scene that Kiarostami mentions specifically

133

as intended to establish a gap between realism and the reality of film-making.

Mr Ruhi seems, in the first instance, to function as a critique of realism in favour of an unrepressed, more 'Brechtian' reality. He stands for the way that even an insistence on real locations and local, non-professional actors grounded faithfully in a social reality and in keeping with the camera's potential for inscribing a realistic aesthetic may well involve distortion. Facing the brute reality of the earthquake, Kiarostami seems to want to set the record straight and establish the difference between a cinema of transparency that conceals the distortions imposed by outsiders, that is, between *Where is my Friend's House?*, and the cinema of *And Life Goes On*. But Mr Ruhi is still not living in his own home; the 'gentlemen' have intervened again and his point rebounds on to *And Life Goes On*, implying a *mise en abîme* in which reality is constantly confused, whether the aesthetic is one of realism or Brechtian distanciation. This kind of confusion between the real and the imaginary is taken further in the third film in the trilogy, *Through the Olive Trees*, from the moment that the new 'director' introduces himself. He then goes over, in character, to a large group of girls to find one who will play the part of the young wife in the docudrama. Local people are cast to re-enact events that had been enacted by other local people cast as actors in *And Life Goes On*.

The encounter with Mr Ruhi is also pivotal, due to its position in *And Life Goes On*. A shot of the director shows him looking from the car window, seemingly torn between his memories of the last film and his imaginative projection towards the next. The film then duplicates this confusion in time. A long track, in close-up, of the branches of olive trees speckled with light and tossing in the wind leads to a sudden shot of Ahmed running up the zigzag path from Koker towards Potesh that had played an important visual part in *Where is my Friend's House?*. Since the path had been especially created for the film, it is emblematic of the imbrication of the imaginary and real. But the path also represents graphically the imaginary line that connects the events of Ahmed's quest, the pre-earthquake filming of *Where is my Friend's House?* to the future, the post-earthquake reconstruction and re-enactments in *Through the Olive Trees*. In *And Life Goes On* the layered levels of time begin to work on the spectator's memory. Farhad's fictional memory, the sudden cut-away to Ahmed running up the path, immediately triggers the actual memory of any spectator who had already seen the previous film. The flashback takes place just after Farhad has decided to take a cross-country detour, leaving the direct roads to Koker, which are blocked by traffic jams and landslides. And the flashback leads, soon after, to the meeting with Mr Ruhi, and thus to his memories of *Where is my Friend's House?*. The spectators' memories of the earlier film are reinforced and, of course, questioned by Mr Ruhi, triggering a movement across the 'before' and 'after' of the earthquake, which becomes a 'then' and a 'now' in the fictions separating and uniting both films. Mr Ruhi then takes the story to his new 'film house', in a small village outside Koker. Here, Farhad stands and watches the people living in ruined houses as they try to rebuild their lives. He meets a young couple and hears the story of their marriage, and the reconstruction of this encounter will be the central event of *Through the Olive Trees*. When *And Life Goes On* was released, the full extent of its reach into the future was unimaginable. Although *Through the Olive Trees* definitely triggers a sense of *déjà vu* in relation to *And Life Goes On*, the exact details of the original scene are hard to remember. But returning subsequently to re-see *And Life Goes On* is to experience, in a sudden rush of recognition, a merging of the future film and the past film in a present moment of viewing.

Over the course of the three films, the presence of cinema shifts from transparent to overt. While the process of film-making is not included in *Where is my Friend's House?*, the director's presence, an awareness of film and its realities and distortions pervade *And Life Goes On*. Finally in *Through the Olive Trees* the story is hung on the production of a film about Farhad's experiences in the earthquake zone. The sense of return, of doubling back, that had characterized *And Life Goes On* is repeated. Mohammed, playing the director, is filming Farhad's encounter with a young couple as they try to make a new life in the ruins, an incident that had taken

And Life Goes On: after the earthquake (*Va Zendegi Edameh Darad*, 1992).

Ahmed's journey: Farhad's flash-back to *Where is my Friend's House?*

Farhad meets Hossein: flash-forward to *Through the Olive Trees* (*Zir-e Derakhtan-e Zeytun*, 1994).

place during *And Life Goes On.* But other realities intervene to disrupt the director's attempts to reproduce this past event. Just as, in the aftermath of the earthquake, the past returned to question the filming of *Where is my Friend's House?*, so, in the third film, the attempt to film a story about the aftermath of the earthquake is displaced by another reality. More and more, the film begins to register the presence of gender relations and the way they are inscribed into this society and into cinema. The film-making process is nearly brought to a halt after take after take in which the 'actors' deviate from the given script. Gradually, the relationship between the actors becomes more dramatically significant than the scene they are enacting and the director's interest begins to turn towards them. The original incident that is being re-enacted for the drama-documentary had not only been emblematic of 'life goes on' but had also suggested that the disaster could break down the rigidity of social convention. In the crucial scene in *And Life Goes On*, a young man had told Farhad his story. The day after the earthquake, he and his fiancée realized that their families had been wiped out ('I've lost many, including cousins, 60 or 65 relatives'). According to custom, they should observe the correct mourning period, a year, before getting married. Instead they decided to get married immediately. He says: 'Amid the confusion, we got it over with', and goes on to describe three nights spent under a makeshift plastic shelter, their meagre 'wedding banquet'. They had then moved into an abandoned house, still largely standing, which the young man was rebuilding.

In *Through the Olive Trees* this encounter is to be re-enacted and Mohammed has to find a young woman and a young man to play the parts of the original couple. Once again, the gap between the original event and its re-enactment opens up an aesthetic vacuum, made apparent first by the static nature of the filming and then by the intervention of the actors' own feelings into the stilted scene. The film crew are in position outside the house and Farhad is standing in exactly the same position as in the original encounter. A young man walks past him carrying a bag of plaster and goes up the stairs. His wife, played by Tahereh (Tahereh

Through The Olive Trees:
the return of the Ahmedapour
boys.

Repeating the past: Farhad
meets Hossein on the film set.

Towards the future: between
shots Hossein courts Tahereh.

Ladanian), who had been cast in the opening scene of the film, greets him, but he says nothing. The director calls 'cut' and they attempt a retake. After two failed takes, he explains to the director that, although he could say his lines perfectly to him, when he tries to talk to a girl he begins to stammer. The director then sends for Hossein (Hossein Rezai), who has been helping out at their camp, as a replacement. Once again, a young man walks past Farhad carrying a bag of plaster. This time it is Tahereh who fails to answer his greeting and the director again has to call 'cut'. After several failed takes, they break for the night. Driving back to the camp, Hossein tells the director that he had been courting Tahereh for some time but, as he had been rejected by her family, she would not agree to speak to him even in the context of the film. Before the earthquake, her mother had rejected him as an unworthy suitor for her student daughter because he was illiterate. When the earthquake killed both her parents, he had tried again, only to be rejected by her grandmother as illiterate and homeless.

Hossein's account goes into flashback with an extended sequence that winds through the crowded cemetery as mourners tend graves in the aftermath of the earthquake. The camera follows Hossein as he watches Tahereh and her grandmother. It is only later in the film that Hossein, in one of his impassioned speeches to the silent Tahereh, says that she had returned his look in the cemetery and that he had taken it as a sign of encouragement. During the flashback, the camera registers Hossein's intense gaze but gives no indication of Tahereh's look. This missing moment becomes a crucial point of uncertainty in the film. It inscribes Tahereh's impossible position, caught between family and suitor. But it also bears witness to the guidelines for the cinematic depiction of relations between the sexes established by the Ministry of Culture and Islamic Guidance. Hamid Naficy has pointed out that eye contact, especially when expressing 'desire', was specifically 'discouraged'.[7] In *Through the Olive Trees* the presence of Tahereh, the first considerable part for a young woman in Kiarostami's films so far, probably marks a point at which the outstanding blind spot of Islamic culture, the status and representation of women, could make a tentative step onto the screen. The absence of her look makes the problem present and her silence further underlines the constraints surrounding young women. Once the filming has brought her unexpectedly into contact with Hossein she maintains total silence, once glancing at him while 'the problem' is discussed by Mohammed and Mrs Shiva. The story has established early on that Tahereh is a strong-minded young woman with a will of her own when she tries to reject an inappropriate peasant dress that the film imposes upon her. While her silence comes to represent the silence of women, Hossein's dilemma is based on class deprivation. He explains to the director that not only does he love Tahereh, but also 'It's much better if people who can read marry the illiterate. Rich people marry poor people; homeless people marry land-owners so everyone can help each other out.' In the flashback, after the scene in the cemetery, Hossein follows the grandmother pleading his case, as they walk through the olive grove, on the grounds that he believes that Tahereh responds to his feelings. The grandmother reiterates her rejection and Hossein wanders, disorientated, into the filming of the drama documentary. He watches a re-enactment of the scene between Farhad and the baby that had taken place in *And Life Goes On*. To indicate the film's new direction, the camera stays throughout the scene on Hossein and only the sound-track and the location suggest the re-enactment taking place in front of the fictional camera.

Under pressure from Mrs Shiva, the production manager, Tahereh agrees to play the scene with Hossein and to answer his greeting. The next day the scene goes well, until Hossein has to tell Farhad how many relatives he has lost. Three times, instead of the scripted 65, he gives the number of dead as 26, the number he had in 'reality' lost from his own family. When Hossein gets his lines right, the shoot is over. Tahereh walks away and the director encourages Hossein to follow her and press his case. Mohammed follows the couple at a distance, perhaps visualizing yet another story about the aftermath of the earthquake in which, out of the ruins and devastation, social barriers might be challenged and personal choice might outweigh family choice in marriage. (Kiarostami worked for two years on a project called *Tahereh's Dreams*, but the film was never made.) The spectacular, six-minute final shot of the film shows Hossein following Tahereh through the fields until he stops and runs back towards the olive grove. Although the ending is uncertain, Tahereh seems to have given Hossein the sign he has been waiting for.

In his discussions with Mohammed, the director, and in his pleas to Tahereh, Hossein often reiterated how important it was for him that his children should have a literate parent to help them with their homework.[8] The problem of homework returns full circle to the point of the trilogy's departure when Ahmed tries to return his friend's exercise book in *Where is my Friend's House?* After the earthquake, the quest for the Ahmedapour boys is the point of departure for *And Life Goes On* and, although in the final scene Farhad and Puya seem to be about to find them on the road ahead, the film ends without them. *Through the Olive Trees* brings the Ahmedapour boys back into the trilogy. They bring potted geraniums for the house that is the film's 'set' and, in a complex, elongated shot, the camera follows them in the car mirror as they run along the road to school. They are safe, but their school, where they are taking their exams, is now a tent in a field.

The earthquake is the central, traumatic and real event that Kiarostami could not show because he was not there when it happened. When he returns to the site after the event, however, the film reacts to the devastation by recording the ruin of lives and homes with a disjunctive style that bears witness to the trauma, while acknowledging the limitations of representation. This separation, or distance, from an original point of reference is duplicated in the way that the film's events are loosely linked together, with extended shots rather than associative editing, which produces an aesthetic of reflection rather than action. There is an element of 'deferred action' in this cinematic strategy, as though a traumatic event had enabled a return to the past, which is then subject to reinterpretation and consideration. Freud's concept of *nachtraglichkeit* (deferred action) attempts to get away from an over-linear or over-determined concept of the human psyche, in favour of a possible revision of events through return, at a later date, out of which memories can find new significance. In his 'return' to *Where is my Friend's House?* Kiarostami blurs temporalities and subjects the film to a kind of revision, but leaves his aesthetic strategy open as though the integrity of events was more significant than closure in the director's images and imagination. In *Through the Olive Trees* the strategy is almost the reverse. The actors who are re-enacting an event refracted through the imagination of the fictional director, Farhad, now directed by another fictional director, Mohammed, divert the past into the future with the urgency of their own story. Once again, the earthquake is an essential backdrop to their relationship, but Kiarostami takes a further oblique step to blur imagination and reality. The story of Tahereh and Hossein, which Kiarostami has devised, takes his cinema through this carefully and casually constructed fiction into the reality of women's position in the Islamic Republic and in its cinema. Although recently, particularly with *Ten*, his cinema has turned more directly towards women, the series of repetitions and returns that make up the trilogy lead towards Tahereh's unseen look in *Through the Olive Trees*.

A Taste of Cherry is almost completely devoid of the presence of women. It does, however, act as a point of transition between Tahereh and Mania, the protagonist of *Ten* (2002). The three encounters in *A Taste of Cherry* are filmed in Mr Badiei's car, closely prefiguring the ten encounters that take place in Mania's car as she drives around the streets of Tehran. *Ten* is filmed with digital cameras, allowing an intimate focus on the interaction between characters and turning literally away from the exterior space of landscape to the lives of women, the interior space of the car and the interiority of emotion. Kiarostami has described how he discovered the intimacy of the new, less cumbersome technology in the 'coda' sequence to *A Taste of Cherry*, identifying his moment of transition at that moment when the use of video was due to an accident rather than design. The transition reflects back, retrospectively, on *A Taste of Cherry*. Filmed in 1996, in the immediate aftermath of the centenary of cinema, the film's drive towards death has an allegorical dimension in which Mr Badiei's quest acts also as an elegiac reflection on the dying moments of cinema. If there is a question of a lost love behind the protagonist's desire for death, it might well be reconfigured as the director's own sense of loss at the death of his own great love, the cinema. The 'coda' offers a possible resurrection and return, phoenix-like, from the ashes with the possibility of a more intense engagement with his society and its problems. But the sound of 'St James' Infirmary' on the sound-track dramatizes a dead love and Kiarostami himself announces that the filming is over.

Chapter Eight
Delaying Cinema

There is narrative cinema in which delay is essential to the desire for the end, elongating the road down which the story travels, postponing the structurally inevitable conclusion. There is narrative cinema in which delay opens up alternative narrative opportunities, displacing the desire for the end. In Abbas Kiarostami's trilogy, delay leads to a cinema of deferral, looking back and reinterpreting the past in the light of later events. In film theory and criticism, delay is the essential process behind textual analysis. The flow of a scene is halted and extracted from the wider flow of narrative development; the scene is broken down into shots and selected frames and further subjected to delay, to repetition and return. In the course of this process, hitherto unexpected meanings can be found hidden in the sequence, as it were, deferred to a point of time in the future when the critic's desire may unearth them. With the spread of digital technologies this kind of fragmentation of film has become easier to put into practice. In this context, textual analysis ceases to be a restricted academic practice and returns, perhaps, to its origins as a work of cinephilia, of love of the cinema. A tension begins to emerge, however, between a cinephilia that is more on the side of a fetishistic investment in the extraction of a fragment of cinema from its context and a cinephilia that extracts and then replaces a fragment with extra understanding back into its context. At each extreme, the pleasures of the possessive spectator are seemingly in opposition to the more meditative, pensive spectator. But, of course, these oppositions are inevitably undermined by the imbrication of the two, there is always a personal edge to the mix of intellectual curiosity and fetishistic fascination.

Finding the 'film behind the film' is the main aim of textual analysis. There is a temptation, similar to the temptation to isolate the stilled frame from its setting in continuity, to detach a privileged sequence from its narrative armature. This is a gesture that dismisses narrative and context and brings the cinephile's love of Hollywood movies into touch with the counter-cinema of the avant-garde. When I first fell in love with the cinema of Douglas Sirk, I saw his films through the lens of the *Cahiers du Cinéma*, valuing his *mise en scène*, his command over the language of cinema, but dismissing his stories as 'trash'. Jacques Rancière's critique of 'The Master of the Universe' section of Godard's *Histoire(s) du Cinéma* is a useful corrective to this spirit. Rancière cites Godard's, now famous, litany in honour of Hitchcock:

> We've forgotten why Joan Fontaine leans over the edge of the cliff and what it was that Joel McCrea was going to do in Holland. We don't remember why Montgomery Clift was maintaining eternal silence or why Janet Leigh stops at the Bates Motel or why Teresa Wright is still in love with Uncle Charlie. We've forgotten why Henry Fonda is not entirely guilty and exactly why the American government employed Ingrid Bergman. But we remember a handbag.
>
> But we remember a bus in the desert. But we remember a glass of milk, the sails of a windmill, a hairbrush. But we remember bottles in a line, a pair of glasses, a passage of music, a bunch of keys, because it's thanks to them that Alfred Hitchcock succeeded where Alexander, Julius Caesar and Napoleon failed: to become master of the universe.[1]

Rancière points out that Godard is not simply extracting these images from their narrative context but also from their place in cinema: the lighting, the shot, the pace or the camera movement that brings them into existence. Furthermore, these images belong to emotion, not simply that of the story on the screen, but the rhetoric of feeling with which Hitchcock plays on his audience's identification and agonized sense of suspense.[2]

When Dominique Paini organized the exhibition *Hitchcock and Art* (Montreal and Paris, 2001) he took Godard's fetishization of Hitchcock's 'things' to its logical conclusion. In a darkened room, each on a Perspex pedestal, carefully lit and placed on a red velvet cushion, were the objects that each encapsulate a certain Hitchcock movie. The experience of wandering around, recognizing and naming them, was fascinating, moving and visually entrancing. But, poignantly, the objects were banal in their extra-cinematic state and almost pathetically ordinary. The brilliance of the display was to create the ultimate tribute to, and exposure of, the fetishistic power of the cinema. These objects, usually transfigured on the screen, powerful signifiers of beauty and suspense, further enhanced by their close association with stars, preserve so much of their original presence retrospectively that they seem to warrant fetishization. But this is a matter of memory and a symptom of the movie fan's characteristic longing to hold on to something from the elusive, intangible quality of the cinema. Looking at the Paini display, even through tears, it was impossible not to remember that nothing looks better than when made from light and shade.

Although objects play an important part in his films, fetishistic involvement in Douglas Sirk's cinema revolves around his style. It would be easy to detach his colours, lighting and camera movement into a cinema of artifice, or a cinema for cinema's sake or to detach his use of slightly marionette-like performances to privilege gestures and looks, suspended in time. But, as Rainer Werner Fassbinder pointed out in his essay of 1971 on Sirk, style is the means by which meaning is made in his films.[3] There is congruence between this style, the genre of melodrama and the process of textual analysis. Melodrama is the genre of displaced meanings in which the 'unsaid' and 'unspeakable' find cinematic expression in the *mise en scène*. The melodrama demands a deciphering spectator who can be transformed into the interactive spectator of textual analysis or delayed cinema. The process of repetition and return involves stretching out the cinematic image to allow space and time for associative thought, reflection on resonance and connotation, the identification of visual clues, the interpretation of cinematic form and style, and, ultimately, personal reverie. Furthermore, by slowing down, freezing or repeating images, key moments and meanings become visible that could not have been perceived when hidden under the narrative flow and the movement of film. Although the alert spectator of melodrama may well have had the ability to read the cinematic language of displacement, consciously or subliminally, at 24 frames a second, today's electronic or digital spectator can find these deferred meanings that have been waiting through the decades to be seen.

To interpret Sirk's use of *mise en scène* within terms of a displacement of emotion from character to cinematic language is certainly valid. But melodramatic *mise en scène* also acts as a means of narration, contributing a kind of cinematic commentary or description, inscribing into the scene significance that goes beyond the inarticulate consciousness of characters. This is almost an extra-diegetic mode of address, reaching out to the spectator who is prepared to find meaning through cinematic style. In this case, rather than a displaced expression of the unspeakable, meanings are encapsulated, materialized and mapped onto the image through the signifying potential of the cinema itself. In certain stagings, Sirk, in common, of course, with other directors, brings into play symmetry, rhyme and binary opposition, building into a segment its own integral pattern. These sequences signal the way in which fiction films are not necessarily structured to move inexorably, uniformly and smoothly forward, driven by a narrative dominated by cause and effect. Privileged moments or tableaux are constructed around an integrated aesthetic unity that is detachable from the whole, although ultimately part of it. Once identified, such segments can only be analysed by means of repetition and return, by the extraction and juxtaposition of signifying elements, by analysing an opening visual premise in terms of its closing. The paradox is that while it would be almost impossible to pick up these aesthetic reverberations consciously at 24 frames per second, once halted and analysed, the meanings invested in such a segment are not hard to identify. From this perspective, there is a built-in or 'pre-programmed' demand, within the film itself, to delay its more obvious narrative continuities, its forward movement, in the interest of discovering these, otherwise hidden, deferred meanings.[4]

In a very different manner to Hitchcock, Sirk makes use of objects or things that are taken out of their ordinary place within a scene to acquire added significance. These objects are given an emblematic status through their framing, editing and melodramatic accompanying music and become signifiers, with an added semiotic value. The audience deciphers these objects as they are transformed into significant images without the help of words. As Jacques Rancière points out, such significant objects are deeply imbued with cinematic value and setting which cannot be arbitrarily extracted from them. For instance, in *Imitation of Life*, when Annie and Sarah Jane first arrive to stay with Lora and Susie, Sarah Jane rejects the black doll she has been given and wants Susie's white one. The sequence ends with Sarah Jane's protest at their new quarters, 'Why do we always have to live at the back?', and she drops the black doll on the floor behind her. The camera moves down, leaving the human figures, following the doll into a close-up, further underlined by the accompanying melodramatic music. With this simple movement, the doll is taken out of its role as a bit player in the scene between the two little girls and transformed into an 'object image'. As the camera holds the shot, it allows a few extra seconds for the spectator to interpret the meaning invested in it. The doll mutates into a poignant signifier of Sarah Jane's feelings, for her desire to leave blackness behind her, for her association of colour with class and 'the back', and also for the way she associates both with her mother's colour. The discarded doll prefigures the way that Sarah Jane will abandon her mother in order to escape and 'pass' in the world of privileged whiteness. Finally, the close-up of the 'object image' sums up the sequence aesthetically and emotionally as its full stop, as a point of punctuation. This is an example of the way that Sirk uses clichés to create readable images with emotional impact that will address the audience directly.

While the object's overstated poignancy may be obvious, even banal, its demand for emotional and semantic response is always fascinating. Inevitably, there is a difference between the emotional impact that an image might have on an audience and how the process might be analysed academically through textual analysis. But both depend on an initial inscription of recognizable connotations, meanings that already have a cultural currency, and their reinscription into the language of cinema and onto the screen. A simple rhetorical flourish, such as the foregrounding of the little black doll, is also a reminder of the cinema's chameleon-like qualities. Not only can it shift from image to image, from shape to shape, but it can also shift meaning from one moment to the next, using framing, camera movement, lighting and music to invest 'semiotic value' into a simple object. The doll's metonymic relation to Sarah Jane shifts into a more general, amorphous, metaphoric figure for the abandonment that her mother will undergo and her inability to escape her fate. While this sliding of significance takes only a few seconds on the screen, it can be endlessly elongated and further enhanced by textual analysis. Halted and repeated on video, the process through which an object's referential status is overtaken by the rhetoric of 'semiotic value' becomes visible. As it is repeated, the image insists and persists so that the repetition and return enabled by the machine are echoed in the image's own repetition of meaning. This process is not only useful for an academic or critical practice, it has its own visual pleasures and rewards that do not replace, but complement, those of watching a film in its traditional temporality and context.

In *All that Heaven Allows*, Sirk adds 'semiotic value' to an object, not as a single point of punctuation but with its special significance accumulating, dispersed across the story's time. By means of these rhetorical devices the audience cannot but see the added value and, as these visual tropes draw attention to themselves, they often provoke laughter at the very moment in which they 'work' emotionally. This reaction marks the gap between the unselfconscious 'I see' and the self-consciousness of '*I see!*' The audience reacts as it might to gags or jokes, for which decoding is not only essential to the very process of understanding but also involves a similar moment of detachment, a moment, that is, of self-conscious deciphering. As Paul Willemen put it, in homage to

149

Brecht in one of the earliest articles on Sirk, these moments of cinematic melodrama distance the audience into the process of reading.[5] He further compares the working of these images to clichés in which pre-existing significance is recycled and recognized accordingly. For instance, in *Written on the Wind* (1956), when Kyle Hadley's doctor confirms his feared sterility and as he walks, distraught, from the drugstore, melodramatic music comes onto the sound-track. At that moment a cut reveals a small boy, riding a drugstore rocking horse and brandishing a gun in an image that is extraneous to the story itself and purely rhetorical. Various themes are condensed here: Kyle's own inability to escape from childhood into fatherhood, the child he might have fathered, his own infantile obsession with phallic objects. The over-determined nature of the image, the vulgar Freudianism, and the rhetorical cinema within which it becomes an element of emblematic punctuation, all register with the audience, which then reacts with self-conscious laughter and the amusement of '*I see!*'

Textual analysis has always generated a tension between a coherent narrative 'whole' and its forward drive and the desire to slow down the movement of film so that time itself becomes palpable. The narrative might not quite fade away, but it falls into the background. It is with this completely altered sense of time that it seems possible to capture the cinema in the process of its own coming into being. A segment extracted from the flow of narrative bears witness to the pull towards tableaux that has always been there in cinema. Now that films on DVD are indexed in chapters, the linearity associated with film projection begins to break down further. It is easier to perceive the lack of smoothness that has always been an aspect of film narrative, its resistance to that forward movement to which it has always been tied by the movement of celluloid through projector. The discovery of a particular sequence or segment that responds to textual analysis necessarily leads to questions of film form both in terms of material and language. To halt, to return and to repeat these images is to see cinematic meaning coming into being as an ordinary object becomes detached from its surroundings, taking on added cinematic and semiotic value. But delaying the image, extracting it from its narrative surroundings, also allows it to return to its context and to contribute something extra and unexpected, a deferred meaning, to the story's narration.

Imitation of Life opens in Coney Island. After an establishing shot of the crowded beach, a complex and carefully choreographed crane movement introduces Lora Meredith (Lana Turner) as she hurries along the boardwalk, pushing through a crowd of passers-by. Leaning over the rail to look down to the beach, she searches for her lost daughter, Susie. The crane shot continues to follow her down a flight of steps leading to the beach, and a man (John Gavin as Steve Archer) positioned at the bottom takes her photograph. Without seeing him, she crosses to the left of the screen and questions another man ('Pardon me. Have you seen a little girl in a blue sun-suit?'). But he turns away without speaking. As she moves back to the right of the screen the crane shot cuts abruptly. The next shot acts as a pivot, as it were, for the sequence as a whole, shifting attention from Lora to Annie Johnson (Juanita Moore). First of all, Lora bumps headlong into Steve, the photographer. In response to her distraught questions, he directs her to the police ('The best way to find Susie is to go to the police.' 'Where ARE the police?'), who are standing on the steps a few feet above her. The camera then turns and moves ahead towards the police to catch Annie reporting that she has found Susie. Here the sound reinforces the pivoting movement: as Steve directs Lora to the police, Annie directs them to Susie ('Right up there' and 'Right down there, under the pier'). The two women's paths cross as Annie descends the steps. As she passes Steve, the pivotal shot cuts and the camera then watches her move away into the space under the boardwalk. The next shot, also still, shows Annie with Susie and her own daughter, Sarah Jane, as she gives them hotdogs, reminds them to say thank you and prevents them from rushing off to play ('Else how's your Mama going to find you?').

The scene has a symmetrical structure. But there are two static shots of Annie to rhyme with the grand opening crane movement that introduces Lora. At the central point of the sequence, the shot on the steps, in themselves a transitional space, mediates between the two and creates the symmetrical pattern on which the structure of the sequence depends. The first and third / fourth shots rhyme, in terms of pattern, and construct a binary opposition, in terms of meaning, around two contrasting female iconographies. While Lora is sexualized and on display, blonde, made-up and white, Annie is domestic and maternal, neatly but discreetly dressed, and black. But the topography of the sequence, its organization of space, translates these oppositions into further, spatial, ones: 'high' and 'low', 'above' and 'beneath'. The particular beauty of the sequence lies in the way the cinema turns these resonances and connotations derived from place into filmic space, turning the depicted location into a pattern of shots, inscribing further layers of meaning, through the attributes of cinema, onto the space of the screen. The sequence ends when Lora enters Annie's 'space' to reclaim her daughter. Story and character take over and, as the movement of projector and narration carry the film forward, the cinematic complexity and significance of this little sequence are quickly forgotten.

The crane shot that tracks Lora's movement along the Coney Island boardwalk starts with a low angle, looking up, but sufficiently close to isolate and emphasize her body and sexual attributes. A close-up of her elegant legs picks her out from the crowd and then the camera moves back to reveal her breasts as she leans forward over the walkway parapet. Lora's emblematic, sexualized femininity is enhanced by the upward look of the camera that treats the boardwalk as though it were a stage. The background to this shot is theatrical rather than naturalistic. The stark, bright lighting and uniform backdrop of blue sky flatten out any suggestion of perspective into a two-dimensional space. In contrast, Annie is associated with an enclosed, as it were interior, space. The wooden posts supporting the boardwalk create a *mise en scène* that has depth and modulated lighting. Furthermore, as she brings hot-dogs to the children, Annie's domestic, maternal and caring qualities are highlighted. The *mise en scène*, the topographical pattern, associated with each woman enhances her iconography.

Annie and the children *Imitation of Life* (Douglas Sirk, 1959).

The mother in distress.

These attributes and resonance are not hard to identify. However, watching the film at 24 frames per second, it is difficult to find time to explore the scene's significance and think about its realization in spatial, cinematic, terms. Once halted, returned and repeated, iconography and topography are easily identified and the scene's integral structure of symmetry and opposition acquires an aesthetic cinematic significance of its own. This sequence calls out for a return to its opening premise, Lora's image, once its closing premise, Annie's image, is inscribed into the scene: woman as maternal and domestic in contrast to woman as spectacle and sexual. But the attributes of place, ordered as they are into cinematic space, not only enhance the contrasting iconography of the characters, but also introduce further meanings. Lora is white and Annie is black. Lora's space, the 'above' mapped out by the boardwalk, not only allows her to be seen as theatrical spectacle, but also, through the workings of antinomy, creates a space of 'above' in relation to Annie's space as 'below'. This spatial opposition carries with it further terms of high and low, so that connotations of class, race and social status merge with those of differing images of femininity. It is this ordering and organization of a 'poetics' of space that make the sequence cinematically special. Its internal rhyming pattern, the beginning and the end, the above space and the below space, invested with values of high and low, is linked by the steps on which the two women's paths cross, when, for a moment, they are in the same frame. The camera itself further enhances this visual rendition of race and class. The grand sweep of the moving crane evokes Lora's privileged freedom of movement as well as the star's entrance. In the space under the boardwalk, the static camera adds to the sense of confinement and containment.

The opening sequence points in two directions. In one, it gives an elegant visual prefiguration of its own story and theme. Lora will become a big success on the stage and screen, spectacularly rich and famous. Annie will be her maid. Sarah Jane will rebel against her mother's inescapable destiny, over-determined as it is by race and class, and struggle to 'pass', to move up from the space of oppression and exploitation into the light of whiteness. Modelling herself on Lora, her means of social transition will be the iconography and attributes of femininity as erotic spectacle. But the film's opening premise also points in another direction. Mapped through the metaphoric significance of high and low, it reaches out beyond the diegetic world of the film into the society to which it refers. For instance, by the time the film was released in 1959 the Civil Rights movement had brought questions of race into the forefront of American consciousness. The pause for thought that comes with halting, repeating and returning to a sequence not only brings with it the close reading of a scene in its primary, cinematic, terms. It is also a pause in which further associations and connections can arise that are, in the case of *Imitation of Life*, unusually rich and rewarding.

The signifying elements in the opening sequence are further dramatized by small details or gestures. The first takes place when

Lora's pose for the photographer.

Lora goes hastily down the steps of the boardwalk, distracted from her surroundings by her distraught search for Susie. Just as Steve Archer raises his camera, she pauses on the step, takes off her dark glasses, apparently to scan the beach, but actually takes up a pose for his photograph. Clearly unaware of the photographer and his camera, her pose seems to speak from her unconscious; that is, her behaviour as aspiring actress surfaces for a second through her behaviour as mother. This moment, and the meanings it brings in its wake, only really find visibility when the image itself is frozen and, once again, there is a time to pause the flow of the story and to think through the implications of Lora's gesture. Such a moment of exaggerated gesture is a characteristic not only of the performance of gender but also of the melodramatic aesthetic itself, with its privileging of 'frozen moments'. However, Lora's frozen gesture is, in fact, a response to the presence of a camera, a still camera that, in turn, itself conjures up the 'frozen moment' of the photograph. Within the aesthetics of cinema, the presence of stillness, particularly the stillness of the photograph, necessarily brings with it a threat to the credibility of the moving image itself, the ghostly presence of the still strip of film on which the illusion of movement depends. Of course, to still a 'frozen moment' on celluloid, on an editing table, is to redouble the effect and to trigger immediately a reflection on the cinema's essential duality, its tension between movement and stillness. Although electronic and digital media cannot generate the satisfaction of such a literal doubling, the relative availability of the technology, and the ease with which a frame may be frozen, necessarily evoke the material nature of celluloid. In this sense, Lora's unconscious gesture reaches beyond that of her character into the hidden, secret nature of film itself and the stillness that has to remain repressed within its unconscious, for its own performance to keep its credibility. Ultimately, this line of reflection gives an extra edge to the film's title, suggesting the imitation that is the cinema and its mimetic relation to life.

The second detail relates to Annie. Apparently, she is the only black figure among a mass of white extras that make up the carefully choreographed crowd in which the child lost by one mother is found by the other. A closer scrutiny of the scene reveals, however, that black extras both foreshadow and accompany her first appearance. The extras are not only on the screen so fleetingly that it would be difficult, if not impossible, to register their presence at 24 frames a second, but they are also placed at the edge of frame. Since the spectator's eye is concentrated on the action of the central characters in the centre of the frame, it is only when the film is halted and the frame can be scanned that these significant details become visible. First of all, in the closing seconds of the first crane shot, a single figure creates a remarkable pivotal point between Annie and Lora, perhaps subtly questioning the accuracy of the antinomy between them. At the very end of the first shot, the camera follows Lora's movement back towards Steve. Literally seconds before the cut, an elegant young black woman appears descending the steps, but only just visible on the very far right edge of the frame. Steve is about to photograph her in an exact repetition of the scene a few moments earlier. But Lora, still 'unaware' of his presence, collides with Steve and his camera. She disrupts the photograph and precipitates the cut. The new frame shows Lora and Steve close together in a two-shot. The choreographed movements of the camera, the stars and the extras is perfectly timed and synchronized throughout the whole of an extremely complex crane movement. Such a shot not only demands considerable pre-planning but also very careful direction in the studio.

The unknown girl.

As Steve turns Lora round to face the police, now standing in the middle of the steps, a black woman extra, with her back to the camera, 'leads' its upward movement to where Annie is reporting that Susie has been found. At the same time, two black extras move through the top left-hand corner of the frame. This detail is, once again, impossible to detect at 24 frames per second. But this moment has the impact of a gesture, not one that is acted out through a character, but one that seems to materialize out of the texture of the film itself, mysterious but present and relevant. Lana Turner's performance of Lora Meredith makes the most of melodramatic gesture and the stillness that it brings with it. Juanita Moore, on the other hand, gives a certain swiftness to Annie's movements, until, that is, she is slowed down by illness in the middle of the film, which then ends with her death. While Lora is blind to her surroundings, Annie is able to read the world around her and the social conditions determined by racial oppression. Looking, rather than looked at, Annie's performance is without melodramatic flourish and it seems appropriate that the film itself should make a gesture on her behalf, associated with but detached from her. Inscribed onto the screen but only subliminally visible, the fleeting presence of the extras relates to Annie's invisibility as the worker on whom Lora's visibility depends. But the extras also have a further significance for the theme of race that is so central to the film. With the image halted, the appearance of the black figures on the screen takes on added power and weightiness, standing in for and conjuring up the mass of 'coloured people' rendered invisible by racism and oppression, very particularly by Hollywood's culture and representation. They also foreshadow the apartheid society to which Annie belongs but is unknown to Lora, because 'Miss Lora, you never asked.' This is the world that finds visibility, filling and overwhelming the screen during the film's final spectacle, Annie's funeral. Here black people line the streets and walk as mourners in the funeral procession and black culture appears with the church service and Mahalia Jackson's singing. The fleeting image of the extras in the opening moments of the film refers to a social unconscious, the 'unspeakable' nature of race enacted by Sarah Jane's rejection of her mother. And their presence also makes a gesture towards the unconscious of the story itself and Annie's place within it.

In Sirk's films, his highly stylized rhetorical tropes lead back into the film's story and then further out into the social conditions to which the melodrama refers. These moments of added semiotic value render visible the despair or desire that traps his characters within what Sirk would call their destiny, the social and psychic constraints that act upon them, from which they may or may not escape. The close-up of the doll, with its melodramatic accompanying music, ends with a fade to black. The next scene fades in to show Annie in the kitchen the next morning, already having assumed the role of maid. The foreboding and prefiguring invested in the previous shot have been realized and naturalized within the story. While Sirk always emphasizes the fact that the cinema does not reflect life, he also sees it as a reflection on life, inescapably caught up with it. As a point of mediation between the two, Sirk uses places, rituals and dramatic moments that are embedded in everyday life yet heighten its hidden tensions. Here, reality, drama enacted within reality, and the highly evocative semiotic transformations inherent in the cinema merge together.

Imitation of Life is a landmark film. Within the history of the Hollywood studio system it represents a high point in the successful restructuring that Universal Studios had undergone during the crises of the mid-1950s. As audiences dropped from 80 million in

1950 to 20 million in 1958, Universal streamlined its production, cutting its investment in film by 50 per cent. While production focused on genre movies that could be made comparatively easily and economically (horror, westerns and the weepies for which Ross Hunter was responsible), Universal also generalized the use of Technicolor. But Universal also supped with the devil. Increasingly, it leased its studios out for television production (Hitchcock's relation with Universal is a telling sign of changing times) and it had been taken over by the entertainment conglomerate MCA (Revue Productions). While larger, more glamorous and prestigious studios struggled, these initiatives ensured Universal's survival. However, this kind of diversification inevitably signalled the end of an era. Hollywood movies would no longer be the single and most important form of commercial entertainment that the world had ever seen. *Imitation of Life* was one of Universal's top box-office grossers ever and Sirk's career, which had only really flourished during his Universal period, seemed finally to be secure. But he decided it was time to leave Hollywood. He retired and moved to Lugano, Switzerland, where he and his wife would live until his death in January 1987. Looking back at this decision, he described his sense that the old Hollywood studio system was coming to an end and that the future would lie with small, independent productions and European New Waves.[6] Although his predictions might not ultimately have been fulfilled, his views closely parallel the line of thought that brought Hitchcock to make *Psycho* in 1960.

While there is no real reason why textual analysis should be tied specifically to the Hollywood cinema of the studio-system period, it is undeniable that the critical practice of close reading has greatly enhanced understanding of 'auteur' cinema. But there is a political dimension to this relationship. The strictly regulated, highly censored and standardized Hollywood that had been, ultimately, imposed by the mid-1930s was beginning to show cracks of unsustainability by the mid-1950s. Sirk's *Written on the Wind* had already signalled Hollywood's new need to be adult to compete with daring European imports and create a noticeable distance from television's family values. And the political climate itself was changing. In a rather similar way to the earlier John Stahl version of 1934, Sirk's *Imitation of Life* belonged to a period of political thaw. Donald Bogle points out that the film of 1959 'hit a chord in black Americans, acknowledging on the screen, as it did, that a race problem existed in America'. However, the depiction of the 'race problem' in *Imitation of Life* still belongs firmly to a pre-1960s, pre-Malcolm X, pre-Black Power era. It belongs to that style of film-making in which a social 'unconscious' is both acknowledged and displaced and in which melodrama flourished. It is, perhaps, for this kind of reason that Todd Haynes's *Far from Heaven* can only mimic Sirkian cinema stylistically, since it is necessarily more literal and explicit about taboo issues than would have been possible in Hollywood even by the late 1950s.

New ways of consuming old movies on electronic and digital technologies should bring about a 'reinvention' of textual analysis and a new wave of cinephilia. But the cinema is deeply affected by the passing of time itself. Now, to look at films such as those made by Douglas Sirk is to have the impression of looking into history. Even studio sets and stars take on the status of document, and close readings inevitably lead to questions of context as well as text. But reflection on film now leads not only to its surrounding history. To see *Imitation of Life* now, after Lana Turner's death and, no doubt, the death of many of the extras surrounding her on the set, is to see time itself caught and fossilized into the illusion of movement. Now, as Lana Turner runs down the steps on the Coney Island set, conjuring up the meanings inscribed into Sirk's film and her performance, she also shifts between the ghostly and the living. Her presence brings with it the cinema's unique ability to return to and repeat the past, which becomes both more real and more mysterious as the film's fragment is itself subject to repetition and return.

Chapter Nine
The Possessive Spectator

Since the cinematic experience is so ephemeral, it has always been difficult to hold on to its precious moments, images and, most particularly, its idols. In response to this problem, the film industry produced, from the very earliest moments of fandom, a panoply of still images that could supplement the movie itself: production stills, posters and, above all, pin-ups. All these secondary images are designed to give the film fan the illusion of possession, making a bridge between the irretrievable spectacle and the individual's imagination. Otherwise, the desire to possess and hold the elusive image led to repeated viewing, a return to the cinema to watch the same film over and over again, which echoes Freud's comment on children's pleasure in repetition, for instance of play or of stories. With electronic or digital viewing, the nature of cinematic repetition compulsion changes. As the film is delayed and thus fragmented from linear narrative into favourite moments or scenes, the spectator is able to hold on to, to possess, the previously elusive image. In this delayed cinema the spectator finds a heightened relation to the human body, particularly that of the star. Halting the flow of film extracts star images easily from their narrative surroundings for the kind of extended contemplation that had only been previously possible with stills. From a theoretical point of view, this new stillness exaggerates the star's iconic status.

The image of a star is, in the first instance, an indexical sign like any other photographic image and an iconic sign like any other representational image; it is also an elaborate icon, with an ambivalent existence both inside and outside fictional performance. The term 'icon', in this context, goes beyond the sign of similarity in C. S. Peirce's semiotics to the heightened iconographic significance and the iconophilia fundamental to the way Hollywood, and other mass cinemas, worked to generate star images. The cinema harnessed the human figure into the imaginary worlds of fiction, but the film industry went much further, hanging its fictions onto a star system. Creating a star meant creating a name, sometimes literally a studio re-baptism as caricatured in *A Star Is Born* (George Cukor, 1954), but always one that could be recognized and named. The star's 'nameability' introduces the third, symbolic, dimension of Peirce's trichotomy of signs. The symbol depends on the human mind for its interpretation, that is on pre-existing cultural, rule-given knowledge, so that the instant recognizability of Amitab Bachchan and Sean Connery, for instance, or Ingrid Bergman and Nargis, would necessarily vary according to their surrounding film cultures. In this sense, the star is recognized and named within his or her spread of fandom, just as a Christian saint would be recognized and named within the spread of Christian art.

When a film industry streamlines its star system, instantly recognizable, iconic screen actors produce a highly stylized performance, enhanced by an equally highly stylized star-focused cinema. Star performance is, not inevitably but very often, the source of screen movement, concentrating the spectator's eye, localizing the development of the story and providing its latent energy. But the great achievement of star performance is an ability to maintain a fundamental contradiction in balance: the fusion of energy with a stillness of display. However energetic a star's movement might seem to be, behind it lies an intensely controlled stillness and an ability to pose for the camera. Reminiscent, figuratively, of the way that the illusion of movement is derived from still frames, so star performance depends on pose, moments of almost invisible stillness, in which the body is displayed for the spectator's visual pleasure through the mediation of the camera. In *What Price Hollywood?* (George Cukor, 1932), Constance Bennett, as an aspiring actress, demonstrates the process of learning screen 'stillness'. After she fails her first screen test due to an over-eager, speedy performance, she gradually internalizes the director's instructions and, on the stairs of her apartment building, trains herself to walk with slow, almost slow-motion, precision down the steps towards a final pose and a lazily delivered line. Female screen performance has always, quite overtly, included this kind of exhibitionist display. But the delayed cinema reveals that the stillness and pose of a male star may be more masked, but is still an essential attribute of his screen performance.

Roland Barthes's preference for the photograph over film includes an aesthetic pleasure in pose:

> What founds the nature of Photography is the pose . . . looking at a photograph I inevitably include in my scrutiny the thought of that instant, however brief, in which a real thing happened to be motionless in front of the eye. I project this present photograph's immobility upon the past shot, and it is this arrest that constitutes the pose. This explains why the Photograph's *noeme* deteriorates when this photograph is animated and becomes cinema: in the Photograph something has posed in front of the tiny hole and has remained there for ever . . . but in the cinema, something has passed in front of this same tiny hole: the pose is swept away and denied by the continuous series of images.[1]

The delayed cinema reveals the significance of the pose even when the 'something has passed'. The halted frame, the arrest, discovers the moment of immobility that belongs to the frame and allows the time for contemplation that takes the image back to the brief instant that recorded the 'real thing'. As the apparatus asserts its presence and the original indexicality of its images, the pose is no longer 'swept away and denied' but may rather be enhanced by the performance of stardom. Pose allows time for the cinema to denaturalize the human body. While always remaining 'the real thing', the iconic figure of the star is ever on display, a vehicle for the aesthetic attributes of cinema, a focus for light and shade, framing and camera movement. The close-up has always provided a mechanism of delay, slowing cinema down into contemplation of the human face, allowing for a moment of possession in which the image is extracted, whatever the narrative rationalization may be, from the flow of a story. Furthermore, the close-up necessarily limits movement, not only due to the constricted space of the framing, but also due to the privileged lighting with which the star's face is usually enhanced. Mary Ann Doane has pointed out that the close-up is a key figure for *photogénie*, the ecstatic contemplation of cinema in its uniqueness, and that the desire for the close-up has traditionally been marked by a rejection of narrative's diachronic structure in favour of the synchronic moment itself. The close-up is thus treated:

> . . . as stasis, as a resistance to narrative linearity, as a vertical gateway to an almost irrecoverable depth behind the image. The discourse seems to exemplify a desire to stop the film, to grab hold of something that can be taken away, to transfer the relentless temporality of the narrative's unfolding to a more manageable temporality of contemplation.[2]

The star's visual apotheosis is no more material than the light and shadow that enhance it so that the human figure as fetish fuses with the cinema as fetish, the fusion of fetishism and aesthetics that characterizes *photogénie*. Here the symbolic quality of film aesthetics, even 'the more manageable temporality of contemplation', leads towards its eternal, unavoidable, shadow, the psychodynamics of visual pleasure. The extraordinary significance of the human figure in cinema, the star, its iconic sexuality, raises the question of how desire and pleasure are reconfigured in delayed cinema, as stillness both within the moving image and within a changed power relation of spectatorship.

In 'Visual Pleasure and Narrative Cinema' (1975) I argued that the cinema, as a medium of spectacle, coded sexual difference in relation to the look while also creating an aesthetic of extreme anthropocentrism, of fascination with the human face and human body. This coding was particularly apparent in Hollywood films, so deeply invested in the cult of the star. The female star was, I argued, streamlined as erotic spectacle while the male star's attributes of control and activity provided some compensation for his exposure as a potentially passive object of the spectator's look. The female figure's passivity and the male drive of the narrative were in tension and difficult to reconcile. As spectacular image, she tended to bring the story to a stop and capture the spectator's gaze in excess: 'The presence of woman is an indispensable element of spectacle in normal narrative film, yet her visual presence tends to work against the development of the story line, to freeze the flow of action in moments of erotic contemplation.'[3]

Watching Hollywood films delayed both reinforces and breaks down these oppositions. The narrative drive tends to weaken if the spectator is able to control its flow, to repeat and return to certain sequences while skipping others. The smooth linearity and forward movement of the story become jagged and uneven, undermining the male protagonist's command over the action. The process of identification, usually kept in place by the relation between plot and character, suspense and transcendence, loses its hold over the spectator. And the loss of ego and self-consciousness that has been, for so long, one of the pleasures of the movies gives way to an alert scrutiny and scanning of the screen, lying in wait, as it were, to capture a favourite or hitherto unseen detail. With the weakening of narrative and its effects, the aesthetic of the film begins to become 'feminized', with the shift in spectatorial power relations dwelling on pose, stillness, lighting and the choreography of character and camera. Or, rather, within the terms of the 'Visual Pleasure and Narrative Cinema' model, the aesthetic pleasure of delayed cinema moves towards fetishistic scopophilia that, I suggested, characterized the films of Josef von Sternberg. These films, most particularly the Dietrich cycle, elevate the spectator's look over that of the male protagonist and privilege the beauty of the screen and mystery of situation over suspense, conflict or linear development. The 'fetishistic spectator' becomes more fascinated by image than plot, returning compulsively to privileged moments, investing emotion and 'visual pleasure' in any slight gesture, a particular look or exchange taking place on the screen. Above all, as these privileged moments are paused or repeated, the cinema itself finds a new visibility that renders them special, meaningful and pleasurable, once again confusing *photogénie* and fetishism.

In this reconfiguration of 'fetishistic spectatorship', the male figure is extracted from dominating the action and merges into the image. So doing, he, too, stops rather than drives the narrative, inevitably becoming an overt object of the spectator's look, against which he had hitherto been defended. Stripped of the power to organize relations between movement, action and the drive of the plot, on which the whole culture of cinema categorized by Gilles Deleuze as the 'action-image' depends, the male star of a Hollywood film is exposed to the 'feminization' of the spectator's gaze. As a film's masculinity has to risk the castrating effect of delay and fragmentation, this form of spectatorship may work perversely against the grain of the film, but it is also a process of discovery, a fetishistic form of textual analysis. When narrative fragments, and its protagonists are transformed into still, posed images to which movement can be restored, the rhythm of a movie changes. The supposed laws of smoothly distributed linear cause and effect are of minor aesthetic importance compared to another kind of, more tableau-orientated, rhythm. Howard Hawks pointed out that a director tends to concentrate drama and spectacle into privileged scenes, so the fragmentation of narrative continuity may also be the discovery of a pattern that has been clouded by identification, action or suspense. But the human body is of the essence in 'fetishistic spectatorship'. Performance and the precision of gesture take on an enhanced value on the part not only of the great stars but of secondary and character actors as well. Movement that looks natural, even chaotic, at the normal speed of film turns out to be as carefully choreographed as a ballet and equally punctuated with pose.

In his video essay *Negative Space*, Chris Petit commented on Hollywood cinema's intrinsic ability, at its best, to produce a kind of 'silent' cinema, a system of creating meaning and emotion outside language itself. There are, he says: 'defining moments that stay in the mind long after the rest of the movie has been forgotten'. He draws, particularly, on Robert Mitchum's gesture and stance in *Out of the Past* (Jacques Tourneur 1947), illustrating the way that his figure is enhanced by *film noir* lighting and shadow. In Don Siegel's *The Big Steal* (1949) Mitchum's first appearance illustrates both the importance of the paused moment in which the star is introduced to the camera and the importance of 'masculinizing' that moment. William Bendix leads the film through its opening sequence, during which he occasionally pauses, heavily lit in profile so that his 'tough guy' image is reflected in his shadow. As he bursts open the door to Mitchum's room, the star swings round to face the camera, frozen for an extended moment in shock, and reflected in a background mirror. This is a moment of the star on display, as exhibitionist. But the risk of feminizing the male star as spectacle is neutralized by violence, by the gun in Bendix's hand and his aggression. Throughout the film, however, shots of Mitchum recur in which his movements are similarly paused, overtly for narrative purposes but also producing a characteristic pose for the camera. Like personal *objets trouvés*, such scenes can be played and replayed, on the threshold between cinephilia and fandom. But in the process of stilling a favourite figure, transforming it into a pin-up and then reanimating it back into movement, the spectator may well find, as in the case of *The Big Steal*, that the rhythm is already inscribed into the style of the film itself.

The fetishistic spectator controls the image to dissolve voyeurism and reconfigure the power relation between spectator, camera and screen, as well as male and female. The question that then arises is whether these new practices of spectatorship have effectively erased the difficulty of sexual difference and the representation of gender in Hollywood cinema. What might be the unconscious investment in the spectator's newly acquired control over the cinematic image? In 'Visual Pleasure and Narrative Cinema' I suggested that, as an active instinct, voyeurism found its narrative associate in sadism. 'Sadism demands a story, depends on making something happen, forcing a change in another person, a battle of will and strength, victory / defeat, all occurring in linear

From pause to pose: William
Bendix in *The Big Steal*
(Don Siegel, 1949).

Pause before violence.

Robert Mitchum:
the star's pose.

time with a beginning and an end.'[4] This premise was drawn directly from Freud's equation of the active sexual instinct with masculinity and its opposite with femininity. Although it was crucial to his theory that the instincts were reversible, Hollywood cinema, as I understood it, by and large inscribed the binary opposition quite literally into both narrative and the visual codes that organized the spectator's visual pleasure.

Among the many critiques of this hypothesis, an important corrective has been offered by analyses of cinema directed towards a female audience. In her study of Rudolph Valentino, Miriam Hansen analyses the ambivalence of his persona, which threatened conventional masculinity but had huge commercial advantages for an industry courting an important female audience. Valentino, as well as other matinée-idol-type stars of the 1920s, upsets my 1975 assumptions about the gendering of visual pleasure. Hansen points out that, as a primary object of spectacle for a female audience, Valentino's persona incurs a systematic 'feminization', but she ultimately revises the unequivocal binarism of Freud's passive and active opposition. In the process, she evolves a concept of female spectatorship that is, in the first instance, specific to the Valentino anomaly, but also illuminates theoretically the visual pleasures of delayed cinema. She begins by suggesting that female vision benefits from being incomplete, in contrast to the 'goal-orientated discipline of the one-eyed masculine look'.[5] Similarly:

> On the level of filmic enunciation, the feminine connotations of Valentino's 'to-be-looked-at-ness' destabilizes his own glance in its very origin, makes him vulnerable to the temptations that jeopardize the sovereignty of the male subject . . . The erotic appeal of Valentino's gaze, staged as a look within the look, is one of reciprocity and ambivalence rather than mastery and objectification.[6]

She goes on to analyse various points at which the Valentino movies fail to conform to either narrative or visual norms of later Hollywood, while the presence of a strong female look within the diegesis grants legitimacy to that of the female spectator. The unusual scopic attention invested in his star presence both on and off the screen is the initial source of this destabilization. In the absence of narrative suspense, activity, physical movement and gesture acquire extra significance, and 'closure tends to reside in smaller units, cutting across visual and narrative registers'.[7] Finally, Hansen points out the sado-masochistic themes associated with Valentino, the 'interchangeability of the sadistic and masochistic positions within the diegesis . . . the vulnerability Valentino displays in his films, the traces of feminine masochism in his persona',[8] which indicate a deviance from the male subject's sexual mastery and control of pleasure.

Hansen's analysis prefigures, at many points, the spectatorship of delayed cinema, the weakening of narrative as well as transferred attention to detail and gesture, and finally the importance of star-presence for a sense of oscillation between index and icon. Valentino's persona, his feminization, his association with lesbians, his possible homosexuality, his foreignness, all add to the uncertainty of both types of signs. In relation to sadism and masochism, however, perhaps the picture is rather different. With the weakening of character identification, vicarious control over the plot is replaced by another kind of power as the spectator gains immediate control over the image. No longer the driving force of the movie, the star succumbs to stillness and repetition. The desire for possession, only previously realized outside the film, in stills and pin-ups, can now be fulfilled not only in stillness but also in the repetition of movements, gestures, looks, actions. In the process, the illusion of life, so essential to the cinema's reality effect, weakens, and the apparatus overtakes the figure's movements as they are inescapably repeated with mechanical exactitude. The human figure becomes an extension of the machine, conjuring up the pre-cinematic ghosts of automata.

The fragmentation of narrative, the fetishization of the human figure, the privileging of certain sequences, all return the question of sadism to Freud's concept of repetition compulsion. Furthermore, the psychic economy of sadism changes in the context of 'Beyond the Pleasure Principle' and Freud's concept of the death instinct. His attention was originally drawn to the death instinct by the anomalous compulsion to repeat unpleasurable experiences, that seemingly contradicted the dominance of the pleasure principle in mental life. Freud reconfigured his earlier theories of instinct in 'Beyond the Pleasure Principle' so that previous oppositions are transformed into one between the life instincts and the death instincts. In another essay he summarizes the process:

> The libido has the task of making the destroying instinct innocuous, and it fulfills that task by diverting that instinct to a great extent outwards . . . The instinct is then called a destructive instinct, the instinct for mastery, or the will to power. A portion of the instinct is placed directly in the service of the sexual function where it has an important part to play. This is sadism proper.[9]

The possessive spectator commits an act of violence against the cohesion of a story, the aesthetic integrity that holds it together, and the vision of its creator. But, more specifically, the sadistic instinct is expressed through the possessive spectator's desire for mastery and will to power. In the role reversal between the look of the spectator and the diegetic look of the male protagonist, the figure that had been all-powerful both on and off the screen is now subordinated to manipulation and possession. Film performance is transformed by repetition and actions begin to resemble mechanical, compulsive gestures. The cinema's mechanisms take possession of the actor or star and, as their precise, repeated gestures become those of automata, the cinema's uncanny fusion between the living and dead merges with the uncanny fusion between the organic and the inorganic, the human body and the machine.

Martin Arnold, the Viennese experimental film-maker, influenced by the work of Peter Kubelka, re-edits fragments of old Hollywood movies and, in the process, transforms the movement of celluloid figures into empty gestures with no beginning, end or purpose. In *Pièce Touchée* (1989) he draws out a man's entrance into a room, in which a woman is waiting, by repeating frames in series similar to the effect of flicker films. As the man enters the door over and over again, as the woman looks up from her magazine, over and over again, a couple of screen seconds are stretched out over minutes. At the same time, the rhythm of the repeated gestures begins to resemble mechanical movements. These experiments accentuate the vulnerability of old cinema and its iconic figures. Subjected to repetition to the point of absurdity, they lose their protective fictional worlds. Furthermore, the repeated frames that elongate each movement and gesture assert the presence of filmstrip, the individual frame in sequence that stretches towards infinity. The repetition and variation of flicker films, as in the films of Peter Kubelka, have no necessary limit but revolve around an abstract pattern. As Arnold combines stretched time with the manipulation of human gesture, he combines reference to the strip of celluloid with the presence of the cinema machine, the uncanny of the inorganic and the automaton.

Some years ago, I digitally re-edited a 30-second sequence of 'Two Little Girls from Little Rock', the opening number of *Gentlemen Prefer Blondes* (Howard Hawks, 1953), in order to analyse the precision of Marilyn Monroe's dance movements and as a tribute to the perfection of her performance. In addition to the artificial, stylized persona, evocative of the beautiful automaton, her gestures are orchestrated around moments of pose. In this particular fragment, played to camera, she pulls up her shoulder strap in a performance of an almost sluttish disorder of dress that is completely at odds with the mechanical precision of this and each gesture. Even though the gesture was so self-consciously produced, it has, for me, something of Barthes's *punctum*, and I found myself returning over and over again to these few seconds of film. In the re-edit, I repeated the fragment three times, freezing the image at the moments when Marilyn paused between movements. In addition to her own precise and controlled performance, dance itself demands a control of the body that pushes its natural humanity to the limits, also alternating between stillness and movement. The developed gesture unfolds until it finds a point of pose, just as the delayed cinema finds such moments through repetition and return. The 30-second sequence ends as Marilyn moved forward into close-up, throwing her head back and assuming the pose and expression of the essential Marilyn pin-up photograph. This paused image seems to be almost exactly the same as the *Marilyns* that Andy Warhol made after her death, in his silk-screened homage to the death-mask. The imaginary superimposition of the Warhol image onto the trace of the living Marilyn has a sense of deferred meaning, as though her death was already prefigured in this pose. An acute consciousness of her 'then', before her death, condenses with the image as death mask and the poignant presence of the index as the 'this was now'.

The fetishistic spectator, driven by a desire to stop, to hold and to repeat these iconic images, especially as perfected in highly stylized cinema, can suddenly, unexpectedly, encounter the index. The time of the camera, its embalmed time, comes to the surface, shifting from the narrative 'now' to 'then'. The time of the camera brings with it an 'imaginary' of the filming into the mind's eye, the off-screen space of the crew and the apparatus, so that the fictional world changes into consciousness of the pro-filmic event. As fictional credibility declines, as disbelief is no longer suspended, 'reality' takes over the scene, affecting the iconic presence of the movie star. Due to the star's iconic status, he or she can be grafted only tangentially onto a fictional persona. If the time of the index displaces the time of the fiction, the image of the star shifts not only between these two registers but also to include iconography constructed by the studio and any other information that might be circulating about his or her life. Out of this kind of fusion and confusion, gossip and scandal derive their fascination and become attached to the star's extra-diegetic iconography. Behind even the most achieved performance, sometimes in an unexpected flash, this extra-diegetic presence intrudes from outside the scene and off-screen, giving an unexpected vulnerability to a star's on-screen performance.

This kind of additional knowledge, combined with the passing of time, brings the 'shudder at the catastrophe that has already occurred' that Barthes mentions in relation to Lewis Payne, the young man photographed just before his execution. 'I read at the same time: *This will be* and *this has been*; I observe with horror an anterior future of which death is the stake.' Watching James Dean, Natalie Wood and Sal Mineo, the three teenagers in *Rebel Without a Cause* (Nicholas Ray 1955), that shudder then triggers another one. Knowing the deaths of all three, which were to come and which have already taken place, arouses the irrational sense of fate that Freud cites as an instance of the uncanny. Overlaid across the indexical uncanny that is derived from the photographic medium itself, in the Hollywood, or indeed any other star system, is this other uncanniness, a sense of an over-determined life, subject to an order and force outside that of the ordinary. But this kind of reverie, moving as it does away from the image, to the semi-reality of biography, anecdote and gossip, ultimately gives way and returns to the diegetic space of the story. The star's image on the screen is inextricably woven into narrative by performance, in gesture and action. In the last resort, the star is on the screen due to the fiction alone, and the iconicity of performance and performer merges back into the temporality of the story. Just as the time of the still frame coexists with that of movement, and the time of the camera's registration of the image coexists with the time of fiction, so the symbolic iconography of star is indelibly stamped onto his or her presence both as 'character' and as index. These different kinds of signification oscillate and change places with each other.

It is perhaps for this reason that scenes in which the star is translated from the iconicity of his or her extra-diegetic presence into the diegesis have a particular impact. Hitchcock quite often used these moments for dramatic effect. For instance, in her first appearance in *Rear Window* (1959), Grace Kelly poses for the camera and, turning on the electric lights one by one, creates her own *mise en scène* as she introduces herself ironically 'Lisa Carol Fremont' to James Stewart, while establishing her fictional identity for the audience. Similarly, in *Vertigo* (1958), Kim Novak pauses for a moment, in profile, for James Stewart to look closely at her, identify her as 'Madeleine', and integrate both of them into the compulsive world of his obsession. These introductory shots are like re-baptisms, when a star's name and image, always instantly recognizable to the audience, are replaced by another name within the order of the fiction. A kind of shifting process takes place. Roman Jakobson has pointed out that shifters, in language, combine a symbolic with an indexical sign: a word is necessarily symbolic while an index has an existential relation to the object it represents. If shifters in language are, therefore, 'indexical symbols', the screen image of a star would be an 'indexical icon', but with his or her integration into the fiction, under a new name, yet another 'symbolic' dimension opens up. The 'naming' that accompanies the star's first appearance on screen is followed by the fictional baptism, but the strength of star iconography often renders this second process partial and incomplete. The three forms of the sign merge in the star system while continually shifting in register, uncertain and unresolved. The iconic representation merges with its symbolic iconography. As an indexical icon, however, the star is ultimately an undifferentiated part of the photographic image, its apparatus and its ghostly trace of reality.

In his essay of 1946, 'The Intelligence of a Machine', Jean Epstein points out that the cinema's fusion of the static and the mobile, the discontinuous and the continuous, seems to fly in the face of nature, 'a transformation as amazing as the generation of life from inanimate things'.[10] Human figures preserved on film embody these oppositions more completely and poignantly than any other phenomenon of representation. The cinematic illusion fuses two incompatible states of being into one, so that the mutual exclusivity of the continuous and the discontinuous, pointed out by Epstein, is literally personified in the human figure on film, an inorganic trace of life. To translate the stilled image into movement is to see the uncanny nature of the photograph transformed out of one emotional and aesthetic paradigm into another. The uncanny of the indexical inscription of life, as in the photograph, merges with the uncanny of mechanized human movement that belongs to the long line of replicas and automata. However interwoven these phenomena may be, the index is a reminder that at the heart of the medium these celluloid images are not replicas but are an actual, literal inscription of the figure's living movements. Furthermore, the cinema has constantly, throughout its history, exploited its ghostly qualities, its ability to realize irrational fears and beliefs in the most rational and material form, along similar lines to Freud's assertion that belief in the afterlife warded off fear of death. While Rossellini in *Journey to Italy*, for instance, acknowledged the long history of the popular, semi-Christian, semi-animistic, uncanny, he also demonstrated that the cinema's uncanny lay in its contradictory materialization of life and death, a trace of the organic in the inorganic by the film. For Rossellini, the more realistic the image, the more closely it rendered the reality it recorded, the more exactly it could catch hold of the human mind's bewilderment in the face of these contradictions. It is when the struggle to reconcile and repress these contradictions fails and uncertainty overwhelms the spectator that the cinema's *punctum* can be realized.

The contradiction is dramatized in the final sequence of *Prix de Beauté* (Augusto Genina, 1930). While Louise Brooks watches, enraptured, as her image performs in the screen test that should make her a star, her jealous husband slips unnoticed into the back of the room and shoots her. As she dies, her filmed image continues singing on the screen, in a layered, ironic, condensation of movement and stasis, life and death, and the mechanized perfection of the screen image. Similarly, the cinema's great icons still perform and re-perform their perfect gestures after death. In the act of halting the flow of film, then returning it to movement and vitality, the possessive spectator inherits the long-standing fascination with the human body's mutation from animate to inanimate and vice versa. This spectator has the power of the Medusa's gaze at his or her fingertips, turning the moving figure as it were into stone. After manipulating the movement and holding the figure in a perfect, sculptural, pose, the process can be reversed so that the Medusa effect is transformed into the pleasure of Pygmalion. This mastery over the human figure found a pre-cinematic realization in automata, celebrated from Hoffmann's Olympia to the mechanical figures that the Marquis collects in Renoir's *La Règle du Jeu* (1939).

For Epstein and his contemporaries, the cinema's easy mecha-

Charlie Chaplin as automaton in *The Circus* (1928).

nization of the human figure was a crucial sign of its modernity, for which Charlie Chaplin was the supreme emblem. Throughout the 1920s intellectuals and cinephiles had commented on the way that Chaplin's performance style captured the spirit of modernity and its relation to the machine. Victor Shklovsky thought that the essence of the comic in Chaplin was his mechanical movement, its development into a series of passages ending with a full stop, a pose. Walter Benjamin similarly:

> Every one of his movements is composed of chopped up bits of motion. Whether you focus on his walk, or the way he handles his little cane or tips his hat – it is always the same jerky succession of

tiny movements, which applies the law of filmic sequence to that of human motorics.[11]

Fernand Léger's tribute in *Le Ballet Mécanique* (1924) is to 'Charlot' as film, animated and integrated into the stuff of celluloid itself. In his film of 1928, *The Circus*, Chaplin introduces confusion between the animate and inanimate directly as a comic gag. First he exploits the endless reduplication of images in a mirror maze, where the reflected figures mock and mimic the Tramp's attempts to escape and the boundary between representation and reality dissolves. Next he takes refuge on a fairground façade where a number of life-sized automated figures perform repeated mechanical gestures. Integrating himself so exactly into the rhythm of the automata that a puzzled policeman fails to see him, Chaplin caricatures the affinity between the mechanical and the Tramp's mode of performance, as well as his frequent encounters with 'things' that take on a life of their own. Chaplin's screen persona celebrates the cinema as an apotheosis of the human as machine and as a realization of the fascinating, ancient ambivalence between movement and stillness as ambivalence between the animate and the inanimate, from automata to the rhythmic movement and pose of dancers. Chaplin demonstrates that Wilhelm Jentsch's uncanny of the new and unfamiliar, so criticized by Freud, belongs to an archaic tradition reaching back to classical mythology. As a personification of the cinema's fusion of human and machine, he also points constantly to its vulnerability, the threat of breakdown, an ultimate ephemerality, which is more usually associated with the threat of castration represented by the beautiful automaton's deceptive femininity. This ambivalence returns for a possessive spectatorship that wounds the film object in the process of love and fascination; delaying it, while also reinventing its relations of desire and discovery.

In '" . . . rait" Signe d'Utopie', Raymond Bellour draws attention to what one might call the 'theoretical *punctum*' in Barthes's observations on the cinema. Towards the end of *Camera Lucida* Barthes describes how he was suddenly and unexpectedly affected by a scene in Fellini's *Casanova* (1976). Watching Casanova dance with a young automaton, he found himself overwhelmed by an intense emotion aroused by details of her figure, clothes, her painted but all the same innocent face, her stiff but accessible body. He found himself beginning to think about photography because this kind of emotion was also aroused by photographs that he loved. Bellour observes: 'The figure's movements, slightly jerky and unfinished with a rigid posture, made its body one with the movement of the film, on which it left a kind of wound.'[12] It is as though the movement of the mechanical figure suggested that of the other, the projector, which should have remained hidden. Barthes prefaces his reflections on the automaton in *Casanova* by saying that he saw the film on the day that he had been looking at the photographs of his mother that had moved him so much. Bellour sees in the description of the automaton the *punctum* associated not only with the 'Winter Garden' photograph of Barthes's mother as a little girl, but also with the body of the very old woman, alive but close to death. He links the relation between mother and son to the cinema itself: 'It may be that the artificial body is always too close to the mother's body.'[13]

Bellour suggests that 'a kind of wound' opened up by the automaton leads to the film's mechanism, to the 'inside', which, like the inside of the beautiful doll, needs to be disguised to maintain its credibility. Film subjected to repetition and return, when viewed on new technologies, suffers from the violence caused by extracting a fragment from the whole that, as in a body, 'wounds' its integrity. But in another metaphor, this process 'unlocks' the film fragment and opens it up to new kinds of relations and revelations. From this perspective, the automaton's staccato, mechanical movements prefigure the hovering between movement and stillness that characterizes textual analysis and Bellour's own pioneering work with film fragments. And she also acts as a figure for 'the wavering and confusion between movement and stillness' that characterize the interactive spectatorship enabled by new technologies. As it penetrates the film, this new way of looking emasculates the coherent whole of narrative structure, 'wounding' the surface. The figure of the automaton returns in a double sense, first as the site of castration anxiety, this time threatening the 'body' of the film itself, and secondly as metaphor for a fragmented, even feminized, aesthetic of cinema. With Barthes's perception of the *Casanova* automaton and with Bellour's interpretation of it, the Freudian uncanny of the mother's body merges with the now ageing body of film.

Chapter Ten

The Pensive Spectator

In the 1920s, for film-makers such as Jean Epstein, René Clair and Dziga Vertov, the cinema opened a revolutionary, mechanical eye that transformed human vision. It opened up new perceptual possibilities, accentuating the changed ways of seeing a familiar external world already affected by the stillness of photography and the speed of mechanized transport. Vertov describes a simple experiment when he

> Did a risky jump for a slow-motion camera. Didn't recognize my face on the screen. My thoughts were revealed on my face – irresolution, vacillation and firmness (a struggle within myself) and again the joy of victory. First thought for the Kino-Eye as a world perceived without a mask, as a world of naked truth (that cannot be hidden).[1]

At the end of the twentieth century new technologies opened up new perceptual possibilities, new ways of looking, not at the world, but at the internal world of cinema. The century had accumulated a recorded film world, like a parallel universe, that can now be halted or slowed or fragmented. The new technologies work on the body of film as mechanisms of delay, delaying the forward movement of the medium itself, fragmenting the forward movement of narrative and taking the spectator into the past. Whatever its drive or desire, this look transforms perception of cinema just as the camera had transformed the human eye's perception of the world. In the first instance, this is a literal delay to the cinema's flow, holding back its temporal sequence, through repetition and return. But this act of delay reveals the relation between movement and stillness as a point at which cinema's variable temporality becomes visible. Again, there is an affinity with the early avant-garde and the aesthetic exploration of movement and stillness as a privileged quality of the cinema. Annette Michelson describes the cinema of Vertov and René Clair in the following terms:

> It is in so far as Clair and Vertov are engaged in the direct manipulation of the filmic process that their finest work resists description. To describe a movement is difficult, to describe the instant of arrest and of release, of reversal, of movement, is something else again; it is to confront that thrill on the deepest level of filmic enterprise, to recognize the privileged character of the medium as being in itself the promise of an incomparable, and unhoped for, grasp upon the nature of causality.[2]

Michelson's description evokes the difficulty of articulating the cinema's varied relation to time, the sense of being beyond verbal language, the thrill that Barthes associated with the still photograph alone. The 'beyond' of verbal description returns to the relation between the photographic index and the uncanny, the inscription of a moment of time then suspended. The delayed cinema, following the cinema of the avant-garde, brings the temporality of the index and its uncertainties, in Epstein's words its 'unstable conditionals', out of stillness into the further complexity of movement and then back again.

For Roland Barthes, the cinema was unable to activate the *punctum* that he found so moving in the still photograph, that is, the presence of reality, of death, the detail overlooked by its photographer and visible to its viewer. He says:

> In the cinema, whose raw material is photographic, the image does not, however, have this completeness (which is fortunate for the cinema). Why? Because the photograph, taken in flux, is impelled, ceaselessly drawn towards other views; in the cinema, no doubt,

there is always a photographic referent, but this referent shifts, it does not make a claim in favour of its reality, it does not protest its former existence; it does not cling to me: it is not a specter.[3]

Furthermore:

The cinema participates in the domestication of Photography – at least the fictional cinema, precisely the one said to be the seventh art; a film can be mad by artifice, can present signs of cultural madness, it is never mad by nature (by iconic status); it is the very opposite of a hallucination; it is simply an illusion; its vision is oneiric, not ecmnesic.[4]

These missing qualities may be returned to the cinema by the act of delaying the image, returning to and repeating certain moments and breaking down the linearity of narrative continuity. Halting the flow of film splits apart the different levels of time that are usually fused together. In detaching the time of the index from the time of fiction, the delayed cinema dissolves the imaginative power of the fiction, as well as the forward drive that, Barthes argues, obscures a cinematic *punctum*.

Throughout the history of fiction film, as Barthes points out, story time has tended to mask the primary, the moment of cinematic registration, and subordinate the fascination of movement as recorded time to narrative drama. For the fiction's diegetic world to assert its validity and for the cinema to spin the magic that makes its story-telling work, the cinema as index has had to take on the secondary role of 'prop' for narrative verisimilitude. Just as the still frame is absorbed into the illusion of movement, so does 'then-ness', the presence of the moment of registration, have to lose itself in the temporality of the narrative, the iconicity of the protagonists and their fictional world. Narrative asserts its own temporality. There is a 'here-and-now-ness' that the cinema asserts through its affinity with story-telling. The moving image tends to have difficulty with the nuances of grammatical time and may fall back on spoken narration to manipulate change in temporal direction and to avoid clumsy flashback devices. Or its temporal ambiguities may be exploited for aesthetic purposes. But all these devices tend to stay within the overall temporality of the story; they reflect on the question of time as an issue within the narrative, whether clumsy or complicated, and the there-ness and then-ness of the film's original moment, its moment of registration, tend to stay hidden.

To delay a fiction in full flow allows the changed mechanism of spectatorship to come into play and, with it, shifts of consciousness between temporalities. By halting the image or repeating sequences, the spectator can dissolve the fiction so that the time of registration can come to the fore. For instance, returning to and repeating the extended shot that introduces Lana Turner at the beginning of *Imitation of Life* gradually creates a consciousness of the pro-filmic scene, the complex choreography between the movement of the crane and the movement of the star and extras, which has a dance-like quality. It also seems precarious, almost fragile in its duration, its registration of the past, and the imaginative world of the story takes shape tenuously, out of the document of a Hollywood, Universal Studios, film set. Halting the duration of the extended take, breaking up its elegant continuity, reveals further details that could not be registered within the shot's movement. A halt on the final slither of the shot, when the young black woman walks down the steps occupied just before by Lana Turner, produces a *punctum*-like sensation at the discovery of this lost moment. Pleasure in the shot's extended duration is replaced by the fascination of an extended pause on a still frame. The sense of wonder at the timing of the shot, at the precarious moment between the young woman's appearance and the cut, then gives way to a reflection on its significance. The near-invisibility of the shot's closing seconds prefigures the issue of the visibility and invisibility of race that runs through the whole film. And that subliminal 'representation of invisibility' leads out beyond the constraints of the film frame to the society from which it is derived. While the timing of this image is inextricably linked to its place within the shot as a whole, it is only when stilled that it can be caught for thought and reflection. But the process of delay also gives visibility to the shot as a slice of moving time, the camera's movement and its recording of movement. This oscillation between temporalities varies according to style. Unlike the complex choreography of a set, the gap between the presence of fictional time and registration time is more immediately available to consciousness when shooting on location, using ordinary people as actors. Rossellini exploited these margins in his use of his stars in *Journey to Italy*. When Katherine Joyce brushes her hair we see Ingrid Bergman brushing her hair; when Alex Joyce smokes a cigarette we see George Sanders smoking. Here a delay in the film creates an oscillation in the temporal clash not only between registration and fiction but between performance and presence. There is an intimacy in some of Rossellini's shots of Bergman and Sanders that cannot but conjure up their own extra-diegetic stories and relationships onto the screen.

The process of delaying a film inevitably highlights its aesthetics and the illusion of movement, and the hidden presence of the filmstrip on which the illusion depends. In his prescient reflection on the importance of the stop in film, Raymond Bellour draws attention to its effect on spectatorship. He describes the aesthetic implications of a sequence in Max Ophuls's *Letter from an Unknown Woman*, in which Stephan looks at the photographs that Lisa has enclosed with her letter:

> What happens when the spectator of a film is confronted with a photograph? The photo becomes first one object among many; like all other elements of a film, the photograph is caught up in the film's unfolding. Yet the presence of a photo on the screen gives rise to very particular trouble. Without ceasing to advance its own rhythm, the film seems to freeze, to suspend itself, inspiring in the spectator a recoil from the image that goes hand in hand with a growing fascination . . . Creating another distance, another time, the photo permits me to reflect on the cinema.[5]

And he then ends with the discovery of the photogramme:

As soon as you stop the film, you begin to find time to add to the image. You start to reflect differently on film, on cinema. You are led towards the photogram – which is itself a step further in the direction of the photograph. In the frozen film (or photogram), the presence of the photograph bursts forth, while other means exploited by the *mise-en-scène* to work against time tend to vanish. The photo thus becomes a stop within a stop, a freeze frame within a freeze frame; between it and the film from which it emerges, two kinds of time blend together, always inextricable but without becoming confused. In this the photograph enjoys a privilege over all other effects that make the spectator, this hurried spectator, a pensive one as well.[6]

Bellour makes the crucial point that a moment of stillness within the moving image and its narrative creates a 'pensive spectator' who can reflect 'on the cinema'. Not only can the 'pensive' spectator experience the kind of reverie that Barthes associated with the photograph alone, but this reverie reaches out to the nature of cinema itself. This pause for the spectator, usually 'hurried' by the movement of both film and narrative, opens a space for consciousness of the still frame within the moving image. Similarly, the pensive spectator who pauses the image with new technologies may bring to the cinema the resonance of the still photograph, the association with death usually concealed by the film's movement, its particularly strong inscription of the index. These reflections are not lost when the film is returned to movement. On the contrary, they continue and inflect the film's sense of 'past-ness'. And the 'pensive' spectator ultimately returns to the inseparability of stillness from movement and flow; in Bellour's words, 'two kinds of time blend together'.

The pensive spectator attempts to translate these different experiences of time into words along the lines suggested by Barthes in relation to the still photograph: the persistence of a present that is now past, 'this was now'. While the same combination of 'shifters' evokes the temporality of cinema's stillness, its registration and preservation of a moment across time, in its duration these moments are continually unfolding in a continuum, in relation to each other as well as in relation to the isolated instant. These levels of time are further complicated by fiction, considered by Barthes to be the 'domestication' of the cinema. Rather than a masking of cinema's essence, fiction can introduce the level of imaginative time that, once delayed, contributes to rather than detracts from cinema's aesthetics. When the presence of the past, the time of registration, rises to the surface, it seems to cancel the narrative flow. In almost any halt to a film, a sense of the image as document makes itself felt as the fascination of time fossilized overwhelms the fascination of narrative progression. But then, once the film begins to flow again and the action takes over, the temporal register shifts again and its fictional present reasserts itself. As these different levels of time reach consciousness, they demand translation into the vocabulary of time – 'then' and 'now' and 'was' and 'is' – that describes the relation between past and present. As Emile Benveniste puts it:

> The essential thing, then, is the relation between the indicator (of person, time, place, object shown etc.) and the present instance of discourse. For from the moment that one no longer refers, by the expression itself, to this relation of the indicator to the unique instance that manifests it, the language has recourse to a series of distinct terms that have a one-to-one correspondence with the first and which refer, not to the instance of discourse, but to 'real' objects, to 'historical' times and places. Hence correlations such as: I : he – here: there – now : then – . . . [7]

As in the photograph, 'the present instant of discourse' is preserved, as though a moment of utterance has got frozen in time, destined always to speak, not in a repetition, but the original sentence itself. With the photographic image, the shifter does not have the sophistication of verbal language, and its significance rests on an iconic rather than a symbolic form. It therefore has to be renegotiated through the spectator's internal utterance that necessarily calls on the shifter. The image refers to a 'real', 'historical' object located in a past that no longer exists. The gap between the indexical 'then' and the spectator's sense of its persistence into 'now' acquires a further dimension with fiction. Furthermore, the cinema's illusion of movement is difficult to separate from the experience of time passing, because the cinema is the only medium that has been able to preserve that particular sign of 'now-ness' into the future. In the case of cinematic narrative, the simplicity and contingency of movement within a single shot, 'then' in duration, mutate to become integrated into an edited sequence and a part of the wider, symbolic, overarching time of the story. Then with a moment of delay, fiction disappears again under the reality of the index that sustains it. These varied levels of time are further complicated by the presence of voice. A voice-over or the dubbed voice adds a temporality that confuses the moment of recording.

Hollis Frampton's *nostalgia* (1971) exploits the instability of the shifter as 'indexical symbol', while also reflecting on cinema's stillness and movement in terms of the 'indexical icon'. In the film, a number of still photographs are filmed full screen accompanied by a voice-over commentary. Gradually, as they are placed on a hot-plate, each one begins to catch fire. Not only does stillness mutate into movement but the photographs' presence in the past also gives way to the moving image's sense of 'present-ness'. As Rachel Moore comments:

> Frampton's method casts doubt on what was there, unfixes the image from its story and places the story, which is, after all, a narrative form in the present, in constant peril of being subsumed by the burning image (that is, the past). In this the film not only enacts nostalgia and melancholia but shock as well.[8]

Frampton not only magically transforms the still into a moving object but also complicates the relation of time expressed by shifters. The 'this was now' of the original photograph's moment of registration literally shifts to a more recent, superimposed 'now' of the film's moment of registration as the movement of the burnt paper on the hotplate replaces the photograph. Another layer of time adds another designation, 'this was now'. Frampton draws attention to these devices by foregrounding the instability and richness of shifter words. Michael Snow reads the voice-over commentary as though in Frampton's first-person narration and each photograph is described over the one preceding it. The voice describes 'this photograph', but it is not 'this' one seen by the spectator. Grammatical tense and the shifter 'this', the 'indexical symbol', are superimposed on the 'indexical icon'. The essentially sequential nature of film is inscribed as the spectator tries to untangle 'this' from 'that' across the series of successive images.

In the cinema, time as it passes becomes palpable, not in the fleetingness of a halted second but in the fleetingness of sequence in process, an amorphous, elusive, present tense, the immediate but illusory 'now' that is always experienced as fading into the 'then'. The specific time that characterizes the still photograph extends into the continuous transformations of 'nows' into 'thens' as the screen image moves forward. As a film's representation of time 'shifts', the stillness of the frame comes to be of less interest than the succession of 24 frames per second. The indexical 'this was now' fuses with time passing, with the 'now' of cinematic sequence that continually turns back into 'then' within a single shot. The protean nature of the cinema, its affinity with metamorphosis, its transformation from frame to frame, is conjured up in Frampton's film. The inanimate photograph becomes the animate cinder dancing on the screen in a parody of the cinema's own stillness and movement, its transformation of the inanimate into the animate. This is the presence of change, in Bazin's words 'mummified, as it were'. The more often a sequence is viewed, the more it becomes an extended 'emanation of an intractable reality'. The already uncertain photographic time meets film's uncertain relation between stillness and movement, movement and change, and time halted and visibly passing. These relations, so beautifully depicted by Hollis Frampton in *nostalgia*, are now more readily available to the pensive spectator with the process of delaying cinema, capturing the moment of mutation in the act and reflecting on the representation of time.

Nearly thirty years ago, in my article 'Visual Pleasure and Narrative Cinema', I described three 'looks' inscribed into fiction film. First, the look of the camera records the one and only moment of registration. Secondly, the looks of characters are inscribed into the fictional time of their diegetic world. Finally, there is the spectator's look at the screen, repeatable across the film's history. For the diegetic world to maintain its credibility and for the psychosexual dynamics demanded by the gender politics of Hollywood cinema to hold, I argued that, by and large, the first and the third looks need to be subsumed into the second. I said:

> This complex interaction of looks is specific to film. The first blow against the monolithic accumulation of traditional film conventions (already undertaken by radical film-makers) is to free the look of the camera into the materiality of time and space and the look of the audience into dialectics and passionate detachment.[9]

Something like this transformation of spectatorship has now taken place. The spectator's look, now interactive and detached from a collective audience, can search for the look of the camera while also asserting control over the look within the fiction. Although enabled by a technological change, this is a consciously produced and actively imagined form of spectatorship that brings related, but different, psychic processes and pleasures with it. The cinema of 24 frames a second produced a voyeuristic look at the eroticized image of woman as a defence against a double vulnerability. Male vulnerability to a castrating gaze could be deflected onto a female body that was stylized to the point of artificiality, like the beautiful automaton representing castration in the process of its repression. But the spectacle of female eroticized beauty also polished the fiction's narrative credibility and distracted from any untoward visibility of the cinema's mechanics. Now, the stop of flow and the eruption of stillness are commonplace in the consumption of film and the fascination of fiction is just one among others. While woman as erotic spectacle could often create a pause in the flow of action, these moments can be held as tableaux alongside other pauses and gestures that have been hitherto barely visible. Furthermore, the passing of time itself affects the body of film.

Film's ageing process and its critical, but benevolent, collision with new technologies combine to give the representation of time, always present in and on film, new significance. The psychosexual dimension of visual pleasure meets the human psyche's anxiety at the shadow of passing time and the inevitability of death. The three different looks that I identified in 'Visual Pleasure and Narrative Cinema' also correspond to three different kinds of cinematic time: the past of registration, the fictional time of the story, and the present, or remembered, time of viewing. When celluloid cinema, viewed on video or DVD, is delayed by the pensive spectator, the presence of the past (the look and time of the camera) finds consciousness in the present (the look and time of the spectator), across the tense of fiction (the look and time of the protagonist). The place of the look in cinema gains another dimension, not stripped of the psychoanalytic but leading to other kinds of pleasure, fascination and reflection. Out of a pause or delay in normal cinematic time, the body of narrative film can find new modes of spectatorship.

Some time after writing 'Visual Pleasure and Narrative Cinema', I tried to evolve an alternative spectator, who was driven, not by voyeurism, but by curiosity and the desire to decipher the screen, informed by feminism and responding to the new cinema of the avant-garde. Curiosity, a drive to see, but also to know, still marked a utopian space for a political, demanding visual culture, but also one in which the process of deciphering might respond to the human mind's long-standing interest and pleasure in solving puzzles and riddles. This curious spectator may be the ancestor of the pensive spectator and the cinema of delay unlocks the pleasure of decipherment, not only for an elite but also for anyone who has access to the new technologies of consumption. Of particular interest is the relation between the old and the new, that is, the effect of new technologies on cinema that has now aged. Consciousness of the passing of time affects what is seen on the screen: that sense of a 'sea-change' as death overwhelms the photographed subject affects the moving as well as the still image. There is, perhaps, a different kind of voyeurism at stake when the future looks back with greedy fascination at the past and details suddenly lose their marginal status and acquire the aura that passing time bequeaths to the most ordinary objects.

The 'aesthetics of delay' revolve around the process of stilling the film but also repetition, the return to certain moments or sequences, as well as slowing down the illusion of natural movement. The delayed cinema makes visible its materiality and its aesthetic attributes, but also engages an element of play and of repetition compulsion. In a reading of an early, 1936, version of Walter Benjamin's 'The Work of Art in the Age of Mechanical Reproduction', Miriam Hansen has rediscovered the significance of 'play' in the evolution of his ideas, particularly in relation to film. She points out that the idea of play allows Benjamin to imagine and conceptualize a relation between modern, collective, experience and technology that went beyond the relation of exploitation inherent in capitalism. He traces the mechanics of play back to children's imaginative relation with toys, with curiosity and, ultimately, the compulsion to repeat. As Hansen puts it:

> Benjamin complicates the mimetic, fictional, dimension of play ('doing as if') with an interest, following Freud, in the 'dark compulsion to repeat', the insatiable urge to 'do the same thing over and over'. Referring explicitly to an 'impulse "beyond the pleasure principle"', Benjamin attributes to repetition in play an at once therapeutic and pedagogic function: 'the transformation of shattering experience into habit'. He thus modifies Freud's pessimistic slant to some extent by imputing to repetition in play a quasi-utopian quest for happiness and . . . with regard to cinema, a liberating and apotropaic function.[10]

There is something of both aspects of the repetition compulsion in the pensive spectator's urge to return to the same favourite films, the same special sequences, the same privileged moments. The dark side of the repetition compulsion is present in its inevitable confrontation with the objective passing of time that old cinema brings to the contemporary viewer and with the now ghostly nature of the image, transmuted into a postponement of the finality of the ending. But there is also a compulsive return to the past of cinema as both an acceptance of, and an escape from, its physical decline and technological displacement. This may be a return to history, for instance to the utopian moments of the pre-1929 end of an era, when experiments with film time prefigured those now made possible by the cinema of delay. Or it might represent the sheer pleasure of the relation between movement, stillness and their modifications inherent in the experience of cinema but so often rendered invisible. Finding the presence of these aesthetics in apparently conventional and commercial film has all the childish and playful pleasure of the treasure hunt. Ultimately, of course, there is a further psycho-dynamic here, astutely described by Annette Michelson:

> The heady delights of the editing table (and the expanding distribution of the vcr, which has, by now, delivered them into the hands of a large section of our population) offer the sense of control through repetition, acceleration, deceleration, arrest in freeze-frame, release and reversal of movement that is inseparable from the thrill of power . . . The euphoria one feels at the editing table is that of a sharpening cognitive focus and of a ludic sovereignty, grounded in that deep gratification of a fantasy of infantile omnipotence open to those who, since 1896, have played, as never before in the world's history, with the continuum of temporality and the logic of causality.[11]

Out of this sense of euphoria, even if only that of the displaced experience of celluloid on to video, the aura attached to the work of art, which Benjamin considered banished by film and photography, returns to those mechanically reproducible media through the compulsion to repeat.

In his video *Negative Space* (1999), Chris Petit records his meeting with the American critic Manny Farber, whom he admired for his

193

ability to discover details and events that were marginal to a movie's main narrative line. The tape creates a dialogue between the cinema of the past and video, between the special insights of a 1960s critic and the new technology that makes critics of us all. This exchange creates a dialectical relation between the old and the new, breaking down the separation from the past from which nostalgia is derived. But at the same time, it is elegiac: there is no escape from passing time and death itself. Towards the end of the video, Petit returns to the comments that Farber had made on a fragment of *The Big Sleep*. Bogart is crossing the street and, unmotivated by plot, glances up at the sky and then touches the fire hydrant as he arrives at the other side. Various extras, including a young girl, walk past him. Petit shows the shot full screen, slowed down and nearly breaking up so that the pixels act as a reminder of the process of displacement from celluloid to electronic that makes the detail visible. He says on the sound-track:

> . . . as the image flattens and becomes separate from the story, it is after all nothing but a brief linking shot, it takes on an existence of its own. And one wonders what someone from a future civilisation would make of this fragment . . . especially the young woman in the ankle socks. Would they wonder what ever became of her? And would they wonder if they were watching something real rather than just a movie?

But the imagined future spectator is, in fact, the actual, present spectator. When the commentary draws attention to the young woman walking past in the background, at that moment her presence suddenly becomes more significant than the presence of the star. After all, Bogart is known, familiar. The hierarchy of star and extra shifts. The young woman, a cinematic document as mysterious as an unidentified photograph, has a presence that would be impossible to perceive at 24 frames per second and can only be discovered in the 'playful' process of repetition and return. *Negative Space* shows how fiction can be delayed and some marginal detail can take on this kind of unexpected significance. In spite of the contrived setting, the young woman in ankle socks also brings the time of registration to the surface. This fleeting moment shows how details, as they break loose, may also activate in the spectator the disturbing sense of reality that belongs to Roland Barthes's concept of the *punctum*.

In his novel *Austerlitz* (2001), W. G. Sebald describes a similar, in this case fictional, discovery of a cinematic *punctum*. Austerlitz, the book's protagonist, tells the narrator of his search for any trace of his mother lost in the ss-run ghetto Theresienstadt and his attempt to find her image in the fragments of a Nazi propaganda film:

> In the end the impossibility of seeing anything more closely in those pictures, which seemed to dissolve even as they appeared, said Austerlitz, gave me the idea of having a slow motion copy of this fragment from Theresienstadt made, one which would last a whole hour, and indeed once the fragment was extended to four times its original length, it did reveal previously hidden objects and people, creating, by default as it were, a different sort of film altogether, which I have since watched over and over again.

In the book, an illustration across two pages shows how the damaged bits of the tape break up into illegible pixelation; a smaller 'still' shows:

> . . . at the left-hand side, set a little way back and close to the upper edge of the frame, the face of a young woman appears, barely emerging from the black shadows around it, which is why I did not notice it at all at first.[12]

Raymond Bellour's concept of the pensive spectator anticipated the thoughtful reflection on the film image that is now possible, a way of seeing into the screen's images, shifting them and stretching them into new dimensions of time and space. The pleasure or poignancy derived from the stilled image then leads to pleasure or poignancy derived from the fragment. The pensive spectator rescues those aspects of the cinema that Roland Barthes felt were lacking in comparison to the complexity of the photograph. Now it is possible for cinema, in his words, to 'make a claim in favour of its reality', 'to protest its former existence', and for its investment in emotional detail 'to cling to me'. Certainly, the cinema is inhabited increasingly by spectres. Similarly, the oppositions extracted by Raymond Bellour that evoke the different attributes of film and photography are now producing new relations and connections to each other, sequentially or simultaneously, out of which new oscillating, shifting, representations of time may be experienced. Immobility mutates into movement that merges with the register of narrative time only to fragment again with a return to stillness and the register of the index. Not only do the uncanny qualities of the photographic index persist, but there is also an even more acute sense that time cannot be grasped and that, in the cinema, 'time that doubles life' returns all the more clearly 'brushed by death'.

References

PREFACE

1   Christian Metz, *Psychoanalysis and Cinema: The Imaginary Signifier* (London, 1982), p. 76.
2   Raymond Bellour, 'The Film Stilled', *Camera Obscura*, 24 (September 1990), pp. 99–124, for an extremely illuminating discussion of these issues.

1   PASSING TIME

1   Paolo Cherchi Usai, *The Death of the Cinema: History, Cultural Memory and the Digital Dark Age* (London, 2001), p. 105.
2   On 25 March 1997, USA *Today* announced: 'The new DVD format gets an official but fitful launch today in seven cities. Stores today start selling the first major wave of movies – 32 from Warner-owned studios. Among them are *Batman*, *The Mask*, *Space Jam*, *Twister* and *The Wizard of Oz*.' With thanks to Deborah and Mark Parker for this information.
3   Lev Manovich, 'What is Digital Cinema?', in *The Digital Dialectic: New Essays on New Media*, ed. Peter Lunenfeld (Cambridge, MA, 2000), p. 175.
4   Ibid., p. 176.
5   Antoine de Baecque, 'Godard in the Museum', in *Forever Godard*, ed. Michael Temple, James S. Williams and Michael Witt (London, 2004), p. 123.
6   Eric Hobsbawm, *The Age of Empire, 1875–1914* (London, 1987), p. 3.
7   Siegfried Kracauer, *Theory of Film*, ed. M. Hansen (Princeton, NJ, 1997), p. 56.
8   Ibid., p. 57.

9   Victor Burgin, *The Remembered Film* (London, 2004), p. 8.

10 Ibid., p. 59.

11 Anna Everett, 'Digitextuality and Click Theory', in *New Media: Theories and Practices of Digitextuality,* ed. Anna Everett and John T. Caldwell (New York and London, 2003), p. 7.

12 Raymond Bellour, *L'Entr'images: photo, cinema, video* (Paris, 2002), p. 13.

2   UNCERTAINTY: NATURAL MAGIC AND THE ART OF DECEPTION

1   In 'Some Surrealist Advice', in *The Shadow and its Shadow: Surrealist Writings on Cinema,* ed. Paul Hammond (London, 1978), pp. 25–6.

2   In *The Film Factory: Russian and Soviet Cinema in Documents, 1896–1939,* ed. Richard Taylor and Ian Christie (London, 1988), pp. 25–6.

3   Vanessa Schwartz, 'Cinematic Spectatorship before the Apparatus: The Public Taste for Reality in *fin-de-siècle* Paris', in *Cinema and the Invention of Modern Life,* ed. Leo Charney and Vanessa Schwartz (San Francisco and Los Angeles, 1995).

4   Ernst Jentsch, 'On the Psychology of the Uncanny', *Angelaki,* II/1 (1995), p. 12.

5   Ibid., p. 10.

6   Sigmund Freud, 'The Uncanny', in *The Standard Edition of the Complete Psychological Works of Sigmund Freud,* ed. James Strachey (London, 1953–74), vol. XIV, p. 242.

7   Laurent Mannoni, *The Great Art of Light and Shadow* (Exeter, 2000), p. 23.

8   Ibid., p. xxv.

9   Ibid.

10 Jentsch, 'On the Psychology of the Uncanny', p. 10.

11 Tom Gunning, 'Phantom Images and Modern Manifestations', in *Fugitive Images: From Photography to Video,* ed. Patrice Petro (Bloomington, IN, 1995), pp. 43–70. Also see Rosalind Krauss, 'Tracing Nadar', *October,* 5 (Summer 1978), pp. 29–48.

12 Sigmund Freud, 'The Uncanny', p. 242.

13 Adam Phillips, *Houdini's Box: On the Arts of Escape* (London, 2001), p. 130.

14 Ian Christie, *The Last Machine: Early Cinema and the Birth of the Modern World* (London, 1985), p. 111.

15 Paul Hammond, *Marvellous Méliès* (London, 1974), p. 89.

16 Ibid., p. 90.

17 My thanks to Daniel Morgan for drawing this essential point to my attention.

18 Annette Michelson, 'On the Eve of the Future: The Reasonable Facsimile and the Philosophical Toy', *October*, 29 (1984). I have also used this citation in my discussion of the Pandora myth in *Fetishism and Curiosity*.

19 Freud, 'Fetishism', in *Standard Edition*, vol. XXI, pp. 152–8.

20 Siegfried Kracauer (as 'Raca'), 'Die Revue im Schumann-Theater', *Frankfurter Zeitung*, 19 May 1925; quoted and translated in Miriam Hansen, 'America, Paris, the Alps', in *Cinema and the Invention of Modern Life*, ed. Leo Charney and Vanessa R. Schwartz (Berkeley, CA, 1995).

21 Freud, 'The Uncanny', p. 245.

22 Stephen Heath, 'Cinema and Psychoanalysis: Parallel Histories', in *Endless Night. Cinema and Psychoanalysis: Parallel Histories*, ed. Janet Bergstrom (Berkeley, CA, 1999), p. 27.

3   THE INDEX AND THE UNCANNY: LIFE AND DEATH IN THE PHOTOGRAPH

1   R. Krauss, 'Tracing Nadar', *October*, 5 (Summer 1978), p. 35.

2   Colin MacCabe, in 'Barthes and Bazin: The Ontology of the Image', in *Writing the Image After Barthes*, ed. Jean-Michel Rabaté (Cambridge, 2001).

3   Peter Wollen, *Signs and Meaning in the Cinema* (London, 1969, repr. 1998), p. 84.

4   Roland Barthes, *Camera Lucida* (London, 1993), p. 5.

5   André Bazin, 'The Ontology of the Photographic Image', in *What is Cinema?*, ed. and trans. Hugh Gray (Berkeley, CA, 1967), vol. I, p. 15.

6   Ibid., p. 14.

7   Barthes, *Camera Lucida*, p. 77.

8   Ann Banfield, 'L'Imparfait de l'objectif / The Imperfect of the Object Glass', *Camera Obscura*, 24 (September 1990), p. 75.

9   Ibid., p. 76.

10 Bazin, 'The Ontology of the Photographic Image', p. 10.

11 Barthes, *Camera Lucida*, p. 86.

12 Sigmund Freud, 'Thoughts on War and Death', in *The Standard Edition of the Complete Psychological Works of Sigmund Freud*, ed. James Strachey (London, 1953–74), vol. XIV, p. 300.

13 See discussion in chapter Two.

14 Jacques Derrida, 'The Photograph as Copy Archive and Signature', in *Art and Photography*, ed. David Campany (London, 2003), p. 220.

15 Walter Benjamin, 'A Short History of Photography', *Screen* (Spring 1972), p. 7.

16 Barthes, *Camera Lucida*, p. 96.

17 Sigmund Freud, 'The Uncanny', in *Standard Edition*, vol. XIV, p. 247.

18 Banfield, 'L'Imparfait de l'objectif', p. 81.

19 Ibid., p. 79.

20 Peter Wollen, *Signs and Meaning in the Cinema*, p. 92.

21 Barthes, *Camera Lucida*, p. 88.

22 Ibid. p. 82.

23 Benjamin, 'A Short History of Photography', p. 7.

24 Banfield, 'L'Imparfait de l'objectif', p. 84. Citing Barthes, *Camera Lucida*, p. 119.

25 Barthes, *Camera Lucida,* p.4

4   THE DEATH DRIVE: NARRATIVE MOVEMENT STILLED

1   Jonas Mekas, 'Interview with Peter Kubelka', in *Film Culture Reader*, ed. P. Adams Sitney (New York, 1970), p. 291.

2   Christa Blüminger sums up the point: 'Kuntzel locates the *filmic* neither on one side of movement nor of stasis but rather in between the two, in the creation of "film-as-projection" through the "film as strip" and through the disavowal of this material "film-as-strip" by the "film-as-projection"', in 'Procession and Projection: Notes on a Figure in the Work of Jean-Luc Godard', in *Forever Godard*, ed. Michael Temple, James S. Williams and Michael Witt (London, 2004), p. 179. See also Thierry Kuntzel, 'A Note on the Filmic Apparatus', *Quarterly Review of Film Studies*, 1/3 (August 1976).

3   Lynne Kirby, *Parallel Tracks: The Railroad and Silent Cinema* (Exeter,

1997), p. 2.

4   Gilles Deleuze, *Cinema 1: The Movement Image* (Minneapolis, MN, 1986), pp. 22–3.

5   Peter Brooks, *Reading for the Plot: Design and Intention in Narrative* (New York, 1985), p. 91.

6   Sigmund Freud, 'Beyond the Pleasure Principle', in *The Standard Edition of the Complete Psychological Works of Sigmund Freud*, ed. James Strachey (London, 1953–74), vol. XVIII, p. 38.

7   Brooks, *Reading for the Plot*, p. 95.

8   Jacques Rivette, 'Letter on Rossellini', in *Cahiers du Cinéma*, ed. Jim Hillier (London, 1985), vol. I, p. 194.

9   Kitano has mentioned in an interview his admiration for *Pierrot le Fou*. Michel Ciment, 'Entretien avec Takeshi Kitano', *Positif*, IV (November 1997), p. 25.

10   Garrett Stewart, *Between Film and Screen: Modernism's Photosynthesis* (Chicago, 2000), pp. 48–9.

11   Ibid., p. 39.

12   Deleuze, *Cinema 1*, p. 43.

5   ALFRED HITCHCOCK'S *PSYCHO* (1960)

1   Gilles Deleuze, *Cinema 1: The Movement Image* (London, 1986), p. 200.

2   Janet Leigh with Christopher Nickens, *Psycho: Behind the Scenes of the Classic Thriller* (New York, 1995), pp. 72–3.

3   Peter Wollen, 'Hybrid Plots in *Psycho*', in *Readings and Writings: Semiotic Counter Strategies* (London, 1982), p. 35.

4   Peter Brooks, *Reading for the Plot: Design and Intention in Narrative* (New York, 1985), pp. 11–12.

5   Charles Barr, *English Hitchcock* (London, 1999), pp. 148, 185.

6   Jacques Rivette, 'Letter on Rossellini', in *Cahiers du cinéma*, ed. Jim Hillier (London 1985), vol. I, p. 194.

7   See Raymond Bellour, 'Neurosis, Psychosis, Perversion', *Camera Obscura*, 3–4 (Summer 1979), for an alternative segmentation of *Psycho* that gives due importance to the opening and closing camera movements.

8   Peter Wollen, 'Hybrid Plots in *Psycho*', pp. 38–9.

9   Anthony Vidler, *The Architectural Uncanny: Essays in the Modern*

Unhomely (Cambridge, MA, and London, 1992).

10   Sigmund Freud, 'The Uncanny', in *The Standard Edition of the Complete Psychological Works of Sigmund Freud*, ed. James Strachey (London, 1953–74), vol. XVII, p. 225.

11   Raymond Bellour, 'Neurosis, Psychosis, Perversion', p. 124.

12   André Bazin, 'The Ontology of the Photographic Image', in *What is Cinema?*, ed. and trans. Hugh Gray (Berkeley, CA, 1967), vol. I, p. 15.

13   Amy Taubin, 'Douglas Gordon', in *Spellbound: Art and Film*, ed. Philip Dodd and Ian Christie, exh. cat., Hayward Gallery and British Film Institute (London, 1996).

14   Ibid., p. 72.

6   ROBERTO ROSSELLINI'S *JOURNEY TO ITALY/VIAGGIO IN ITALIA* (1953)

1   Robin Wood: 'Ingrid Bergman on Roberto Rossellini', *Film Comment*, 10 (July–August 1974), p. 14.

2   The method was devised by Giuseppe Fiorelli, archaeologist and supporter of the Carbonari movement for a united Italy, who was put in charge of the excavations in 1860 by Victor Emmanuel.

3   Raymond Bellour, 'The Film Stilled', *Camera Obscura*, 24 (September 1990), p. 109.

4   It is important to remember Rossellini's dedication in his later television work to understanding and conveying the ideas of both antiquity and Enlightenment.

5   Anthony Vidler, *The Architectural Uncanny: Essays in the Modern Unhomely* (Cambridge, MA, 1992), p. 47.

6   The name of the couple, 'Joyce', may well be a tribute to the story.

7   The sudden disruption of a relationship between husband and wife by a slight detail that provokes the husband's jealousy is common to both 'The Dead' and Colette's *Duo*, Rossellini's original project for Bergman and Sanders.

8   D. N. Rodowick, *Gilles Deleuze's Time Machine* (Durham, NC, 1997), p. 13.

9   Rossellini identified with laziness. In *Quasi un'autobiografia* (Milan, 1987), p. 54, he tells this story of an American haranguing a Neapolitan: 'What are you doing?'

'Nothing.'

'You should work.'

'What for?'

'You could earn money.'

'What for?'

'You could get married and have children.'

'What for?'

'Then they would take care of you and you could rest.'

'That's just what I'm doing now.'

10 Giuliana Bruno, *Streetwalking on a Ruined Map: Cultural Theory in the City Films of Elvira Notari* (Princeton, NJ, 1993), p. 210.

11 Tag Gallagher, *The Adventures of Roberto Rossellini: His Life and Films* (New York, 1996), pp. 398–9.

12 Maurice Schrerer (Eric Rohmer) and François Truffaut, 'Interview with Roberto Rossellini', *Cahiers du Cinéma*, 37 (July 1954).

13 See Norman Lewis, *Naples '44: An Intelligence Officer in the Italian Labyrinth* (London, 1983), pp. 104–8, for an account of an eruption of Vesuvius and the role of San Gennaro during 1944.

14 These giant sculptures, Roman copies of Greek originals, had been made originally to stand in the Baths of Caracalla in Rome as spectacular decorative features. They were brought to Naples by Charles, founder of the Bourbon dynasty, in the eighteenth century.

15 Rosselini, *Quasi un'autobiografia*, p. 63.

16 This 'juxtaposition' between locations follows a narrative thematic logic, not geography.

7 ABBAS KIAROSTAMI: CINEMA OF UNCERTAINTY, CINEMA OF DELAY

1 Michel Ciment, 'Entretien avec Abbas Kiarostami', *Positif*, 442 (December 1997), p. 84.

2 Peter Brooks, *Reading for the Plot: Design and Intention in Narrative* (New York, 1984), p. 104.

3 Stephane Goudet, 'La Reprise: retour sur l'ensemble de l'œuvre de Abbas Kiarostami', *Positif*, 408 (February 1995), p. 12.

4 Gilles Deleuze, *Cinema 2: The Time Image* (London, 1989), p. 272.

5 An influential moment, often referred to, had been a retrospective of Italian neo-realism held in Tehran in the 1960s. Kiarostami has

mentioned his admiration for Rossellini: 'I often went to the cinema when I was young and I was profoundly marked by Italian Neo-realism, particularly Rossellini. There are clear connections between the ruins and the people in *Germany Year Zero* and those of *And Life Goes On*. But during the whole time of writing and filming I never thought about it.' *Positif*, 380 (October 1992), p. 32. In 1992 he received the Prix Rossellini at Cannes for *And Life Goes On*.

6   André Bazin, 'The Evolution of the Language of Cinema', *What is Cinema?* (Berkeley, CA, 1967), vol. I, p. 37.

7   Hamid Naficy, 'Islamicising Film Culture in Iran', in *The New Iranian Cinema: Politics, Representation and Identity*, ed. Richard Tapper (London, 2002), p. 46.

8   In 1989, Kirostami made a documentary, *Homework*, that elaborates on the problem through interviews with children

8   DELAYING CINEMA

1   Jean-Luc Godard: *Histoire(s) du cinéma* (Munich, 1999), pp. 42–3.

2   Jacques Rancière, *La fable cinématographique* (Paris, 2001), p. 220.

3   R. W. Fassbinder, 'Six Films by Douglas Sirk', in *Douglas Sirk*, ed. Laura Mulvey and Jon Halliday (Edinburgh, 1971).

4   The importance of the segment for textual analysis of Hollywood cinema was established particularly through Raymond Bellour's engagement with Christian Metz's pioneering analyses. See Raymond Bellour, 'The Obvious and the Code', *Screen*, xv/4 (Winter 1974–5).

5   Paul Willemen, 'Distanciation and Douglas Sirk', *Screen*, xii/2 (Summer 1971), pp. 63–7.

6   Jon Halliday, *Sirk on Sirk* (London, 1972).

9   THE POSSESSIVE SPECTATOR

1   Roland Barthes, *Camera Lucida* (London, 1993), p. 78.

2   Mary Ann Doane, 'The Close-up: Scale and Detail in the Cinema', *Differences: A Journal of Feminist Cultural Studies*, xiv/3 (Fall 2003), p. 97.

3   Laura Mulvey, 'Visual Pleasure and Narrative Cinema', in *Visual and Other Pleasures* (London, 1989), p. 19.

4   Ibid., p. 22.

5   Miriam Hansen, *Babel and Babylon: Spectatorship in American Silent Film* (Cambridge, MA, 1991), p. 278.

6   Ibid., p. 279.

7   Ibid., p. 282.

8   Ibid., p. 287.

9   Sigmund Freud, 'The Economic Problem of Masochism', in *The Standard Edition of the Complete Psychological Works of Sigmund Freud*, ed. James Strachey (London, 1953–74), vol. XIX, pp. 159–70.

10 Jean Epstein, 'The Intelligence of a Machine', *Ecrits sur le cinéma* (Paris, 1974), p. 259.

11 Quoted from Benjamin's draft notes for the Art Work Essay in Miriam Hansen, 'Room for Play: Benjamin's Gamble with Cinema', *Canadian Revue of Film Studies/Revue Canadienne d'Etudes Cinématographique*, XIII/1 (2003), p. 5 [The Martin Walsh Memorial Lecture, 2003].

12 Raymond Bellour, "'. . . rait" Signe d'utopie', in 'Roland Barthes d'après Roland Barthes', *Rue Descartes*, 34 (December 2001), p. 43.

13 Ibid., p. 43.

10 THE PENSIVE SPECTATOR

1   Dziga Vertov, 'Kino Eye' in *Film Makers on Film Making*, ed. Harry M. Geduld (Bloomington, IN, and London, 1967), p. 91.

2   Annette Michelson: 'From Magician to Epistomologist: Vertov's *The Man with a Movie Camera*', in *The Essential Cinema*, ed. P. Adams Sitney (New York, 1975), p. 104.

3   Roland Barthes, *Camera Lucida* (London, 1993), p. 89.

4   Ibid., p. 117.

5   Raymond Bellour, 'The Pensive Spectator', *Wide Angle*, vol. IX/1, pp. 6–7.

6   Ibid., p. 10.

7   Emile Benveniste, *Problems in General Linguistics* (Coral Gables, FL, 1971), p. 219.

8   Rachel O. Moore, *Savage Theory: Cinema as Modern Magic* (Durham, NC, and London, 2000), p. 150.

9   Laura Mulvey, 'Visual Pleasure and Narrative Cinema', in *Visual and Other Pleasures* (London, 1989), p. 26.

10 Miriam Hansen, 'Room for Play: Benjamin's Gamble with Cinema',

Canadian Revue of Film Studies/Revue Canadienne d'Etudes Cinématographique, XIII/1 (2003), p. 5 [The Martin Walsh Memorial Lecture, 2003].

11   Annette Michelson, 'The Kinetic Icon in the Work of Mourning', *October*, 52 (Spring 1990), pp. 22–3.

12   W. G. Sebald, *Austerlitz*, trans. Anthea Bell (London, 2001), p. 345.

Bibliography

Andrew, Geoff, *10* (London, 2005)

Banfield, Ann, 'L'Imparfait de l'objectif: The Imperfect of the Object Glass', *Camera Obscura*, 24 (September 1990)

Barr, Charles, *English Hitchcock* (London, 1999)

Barthes, Roland, *Camera Lucida* (London, 1993)

Bazin, André, 'The Ontology of the Photographic Image', in *What is Cinema?*, ed. and trans. Hugh Gray (Berkeley, CA, 1967), vol. I

Bellour, Raymond, *L'Entr'images: photo, cinema, video* (Paris, 2002)

—, 'Neurosis, Psychosis, Perversion', *Camera Obscura*, 3–4 (Summer 1979)

—, 'The Pensive Spectator', *Wide Angle*, IX/1 (1987), p. 6

—, '" . . . rait" Signe d'utopie', in 'Roland Barthes d'après Roland Barthes', *Rue Descartes*, 34 (December 2001)

—, 'The Film Stilled', *Camera Obscura*, 24 (September 1990)

Benjamin, Walter, 'A Short History of Photography', *Screen* (Spring 1972)

Benveniste, Emile, *Problems in General Linguistics* (Coral Gables, FL, 1971)

Bruno, Giuliana, *Streetwalking on a Ruined Map: Cultural Theory in the City Films of Elvira Notari* (Princeton, NJ, 1993)

Burgin, Victor, *The Remembered Film* (London, 2004)

Christie, Ian, *The Last Machine: Early Cinema and the Birth of the Modern World* (London, 1985)

Crary, Jonathan, *Techniques of the Observer* (Cambridge, MA, 1990)

Deleuze, Gilles, *Cinema 1: The Movement Image* (Minneapolis, MN, 1986)

—, *Cinema 2: The Time Image* (London, 1989)

Doane, Mary Ann, 'The Close-up: Scale and Detail in the Cinema', *Differences: A Journal of Feminist Cultural Studies*, XIV/3 (Fall, 2003)

Epstein, Jean, 'The Intelligence of a Machine', in *Ecrits sur le cinéma* (Paris, 1974)

Everett, Anna, 'Digitextuality and Click Theory', in *New Media: Theories and Practices of Digitextuality*, ed. Anna Everett and John T. Caldwell (New York and London, 2003)

Fassbinder, R. W., 'Six Films by Douglas Sirk', in *Douglas Sirk*, ed. Laura Mulvey and Jon Halliday (Edinburgh, 1971).

Freud, Sigmund, 'Beyond the Pleasure Principle', in *The Standard Edition of the Complete Psychological Works of Sigmund Freud*, ed. James Strachey (London, 1953–74), vol. XIV

—, 'The Economic Problem of Masochism', in *The Standard Edition of the Complete Psychological Works of Sigmund Freud*, ed. James Strachey (London, 1953–74), vol. XIX

—, 'Thoughts on War and Death', in *The Standard Edition of the Complete Psychological Works of Sigmund Freud*, ed. James Strachey (London, 1953–74), vol. XIV

—, 'The Uncanny', in *The Standard Edition of the Complete Psychological Works of Sigmund Freud*, ed. James Strachey (London, 1953–74), vol. XIV

Gallagher, Tag, *The Adventures of Roberto Rossellini: His Life and Films* (New York, 1996)

Halliday, Jon, *Sirk on Sirk* (London, 1972)

Paul Hammond, ed., *The Shadow and its Shadow: Surrealist Writings on Cinema* (London, 1978)

Hammond, Paul, *Marvellous Méliès* (London, 1974)

Hansen, Miriam, *Babel and Babylon: Spectatorship in American Silent Film* (Cambridge, MA, 1991)

—, 'Room for Play: Benjamin's Gamble with Cinema', *Canadian Revue of Film Studies/Revue Canadienne d'Etudes Cinématographique*, XIII/1 (2003)

Heath, Stephen, 'Cinema and Psychoanalysis: Parallel Histories', in *Endless Night. Cinema and Psychoanalysis: Parallel Histories*, ed. Janet Bergstrom (Berkeley, CA, 1999)

Hillier, Jim, ed., *Cahiers du Cinéma. The 1950s: Neo-Realism, Hollywood, New Wave* (London, 1985)

Hobsbawm, Eric, *The Age of Empire, 1875–1914* (London, 1987)

Jentsch, Ernst, 'On the Psychology of the Uncanny' [1906], *Angelaki*, II/1 (1995).

Kermode, Frank, *The Sense of the End: Studies in the Theory of Fiction* (London, 1967)

Kirby, Lynne, *Parallel Tracks: The Railroad and Silent Cinema* (Exeter, 1997)

Kracauer, Siegfried, *Theory of Film*, ed. M. Hansen (Princeton, NJ, 1997)

Krauss, Rosalind, 'Tracing Nadar', *October*, 5 (1978)

Kuntzel, Thierry, 'A Note on the Filmic Apparatus', *Quarterly Review of Film Studies*, I/3 (August 1976)

Mannoni, Laurent, *The Great Art of Light and Shadow* (Exeter, 2000)

Manovich, Lev, 'What is Digital Cinema?', in *The Digital Dialectic: New Essays on New Media*, ed. Peter Lunenfeld (Cambridge, MA, 2000)

Mekas, Jonas, 'Interview with Peter Kubelka', in *Film Culture Reader*, ed. P. Adams Sitney (New York, 1970)

Metz, Christian, *Psychoanalysis and Cinema: The Imaginary Signifier* (London, 1982)

Michelson, Annette, 'From Magician to Epistemologist: Vertov's *The Man with a Movie Camera*', in *The Essential Cinema*, ed. P. Adams Sitney (New York, 1975)

—, 'The Kinetic Icon in the Work of Mourning', *October*, 52 (Spring 1990)

—, 'On the Eve of the Future: The Reasonable Facsimile and the Philosophical Toy', *October*, 29 (1984)

Moore, Rachel O., *Savage Theory: Cinema as Modern Magic* (Durham, NC, and London, 2000)

Mulvey, Laura, 'Visual Pleasure and Narrative Cinema', in *Visual and Other Pleasures* (London, 1989)

Naficy, Hamid, 'Islamicising Film Culture in Iran', in *The New Iranian Cinema: Politics, Representation and Identity*, ed. Richard Tapper (London, 2002)

Phillips, Adam, *Houdini's Box: On the Arts of Escape* (London, 2001)

Rancière, Jacques, *La fable cinematographique* (Paris, 2001)

Rodowick, D. N., *Gilles Deleuze's Time Machine* (Durham, NC, 1997)

Rossellini, Roberto, *Quasi un'autobiografia* (Milan, 1987)

Schrerer, Maurice (Eric Rohmer) and François Truffaut, 'Interview with Roberto Rossellini', *Cahiers du Cinéma*, 37 (July 1954)

Schwartz, Vanessa, 'Cinematic Spectatorship before the Apparatus: The Public Taste for Reality in *fin-de siècle* Paris', in *Cinema and the Invention of Modern Life*, ed. Leo Charney and Vanessa Schwartz (San Francisco and Los Angeles, 1995)

Sebald, W. G., *Austerlitz*, trans. Anthea Bell (London, 2001)

Stewart, Garrett, *Between Film and Screen: Modernism's Photosynthesis* (Chicago, 2000)

Taubin, Amy, 'Douglas Gordon', in *Spellbound: Art and Film*, ed. Philip Dodd and Ian Christie, exh. cat., Hayward Gallery and British Film Institute (London, 1996).

Taylor, Richard, and Ian Christie, eds, *The Film Factory: Russian and Soviet Cinema in Documents, 1896–1939* (London, 1988)

Temple, Michael, James S. Williams and Michael Witt, eds, *Forever Godard*, (London, 2004)

Usai, Paolo Cherchi, *The Death of the Cinema: History, Cultural Memory and the Digital Dark Age* (London, 2001)

Vaughan, Dai, *Let There Be Lumière: Studies in the Documentary* (London, 1999)

Vidler, Anthony, *The Architectural Uncanny: Essays in the Modern Unhomely* (Cambridge, MA, and London, 1992)

Willemen, Paul, 'Distanciation and Douglas Sirk', *Screen*, XII/2 (Summer 1971)

Wollen, Peter, 'Hybrid Plots in *Psycho*', in *Readings and Writings: Semiotic Counter Strategies* (London, 1982)

—, *Signs and Meaning in the Cinema* (London, 1969, repr. 1998)

Wood, Robin, 'Ingrid Bergman on Roberto Rossellini', *Film Comment*, 10 (July–August 1974)

Acknowledgements

I gratefully acknowledge a grant from the Arts and Humanities Research Council that enabled me to take sabbatical leave (Spring 2004), during which I was able to consolidate my work on this book. I am grateful to Mandy Merck and Marquard Smith for reading and commenting on the book in draft form and to Ian Christie for his help and advice. My thanks to Kelly Robinson for research and to my sister, Rosamund Howe, for her expert editing of the final manuscript.

Index